The New Civilisation

Anastasia herself has stated that this book consists of words and phrases in combinations *which have a beneficial effect on the reader.* This has been attested by the letters received to date from tens of thousands of readers all over the world.

If you wish to gain as full an appreciation as possible of the ideas, thoughts and images set forth here, as well as experience the benefits that come with this appreciation, we recommend you find a quiet place for your reading where there is the least possible interference from artificial noises (motor traffic, radio, TV, household appliances etc.). *Natural sounds,* on the other hand — the singing of birds, for example, or the patter of rain, or the rustle of leaves on nearby trees — may be a welcome accompaniment to the reading process.

The New Civilisation

Vladimir Megré

Translated from the Russian by **John Woodsworth**
Edited by **Dr Leonid Sharashkin**

RINGING
CEDARS
PRESS

KAHULUI • HAWAII • USA

Mixed Sources
Product group from well-managed
forests and other controlled sources
www.fsc.org Cert no. SW-COC-002283
© 1996 Forest Stewardship Council
FSC

Printed on 100% post-consumer recycled paper

Publisher's Cataloging-In-Publication Data

Megre, V. (Vladimir), 1950-
  [Nova´i`a ´t`siviliza´t`si´i`a. English.]
  The new civilisation / Vladimir Megré ; translated from the Russian by
John Woodsworth ; edited by Leonid Sharashkin. — 2nd ed., rev.

  p. ; cm. — (The ringing cedars series ; bk. 8, pt. 1)

  ISBN: 978-0-9801812-7-2

  1. Spirituality. 2. Nature—Religious aspects. 3. Human ecology. I.
Woodsworth, John, 1944- II. Sharashkin, Leonid. III. Title. IV. Title:
Nova´i`a ´t`siviliza´t`si´i`a. English. V. Series: Megre, V. (Vladimir), 1950-
Ringing cedars series, bk. 8, pt. 1.

GF80 .M44 2008h
304.2   2008923353

Contents

CHAPTER ONE

Pre-dawn feelings

Anastasia was still asleep. And over the endless Siberian taiga the first glow of light was breaking across the pre-dawn sky. This time I was the first to waken, but stayed quietly lying beside her on my sleeping bag, admiring her serene and beautiful face and the flowing contours of her figure, as the soft, heavenly light of the advancing morning made them ever more distinct. It was good that this time she had arranged for us to spend the night under the open sky. She had no doubt been able to sense the warmth and gentle stillness of the approaching night, and so had made our bed not in her cozy dug-out cave but outdoors, at its entrance. She had spread out my sleeping bag, which I had brought during a previous visit to the taiga, while she fixed up beside me a beautiful place to sleep for herself, comprised of flowers and dried grasses.

She looked picture-perfect lying there on that taiga bed, wearing a thin flaxen knee-length dress, which I had brought her as a gift from my readers. Perhaps she put it on only when I was around; she was quite capable of sleeping in the nude. The colder it was in the forest, the more dried grasses were applied; after all, a haystack can keep out the cold in the winter too. Even a simple soul without Anastasia's level of hardiness could sleep comfortably in hay without extra clothing. I tried it myself. But this time I was lying there on my sleeping bag, looking at Anastasia resting beside me, and I kept imagining how this whole scene might look in a wide-screen feature film.

A sylvan glade in the depths of the endless Siberian taiga. The pre-dawn stillness is only rarely broken by a scarcely audible rustling of branches in the crowns of the majestic cedars. And here is this beautiful woman so serenely asleep on her bed of grasses and flowers. Her breathing is perfectly even and barely audible. The only thing noticeable is the slight swaying to and fro of a blade of grass clinging to her upper lip as she inhales and exhales the health-giving air of the Siberian taiga.

Never before had I managed to see Anastasia asleep here — she was always the first to awake. But this time...

I took great delight in watching her. Carefully raising my upper body and resting on my elbow, I studied her face, immersed myself in thought and began talking to myself.

You are still altogether beautiful, Anastasia. It will soon be ten years that we have known each other. Of course I've got older during this time, while you've hardly changed at all. No wrinkles on your face. Only your golden hair is now showing one strand of silver grey. Apparently something extraordinary's happened to you. Judging by the massive campaign that's been unleashed against you and your ideas, judging by what is being said in the press and bureaucrats' offices, something is going on in the dark forces' camp. They keep trying to get on my nerves, and I know how they'd love to get their hands on you. But their arms are evidently not long enough...

And still, you've got that grey strand of hair showing. But it can't spoil your extraordinary beauty. You know, tinting individual strands a variety of colours is an 'in' thing right now. Among our young people today highlighting strands is a hip fashion statement. And you don't even need to go to a hairdresser's — it's just happened all on its own. And the scar where that bullet grazed you,[1] it's practically gone.

[1] See Book 3, Chapter 7: "Assault!".

The pre-dawn sky continued to brighten, and the scar was barely noticeable, even up close. Soon it would disappear completely.

Look at you sleeping so peacefully here in the fresh air, in your own taiga world, while out there, in our world, extremely significant events are taking place. Researchers are talking about an 'information revolution'. Perhaps it is thanks to you, or perhaps they are simply following the dictates of their own hearts, but people in our technocratic world are beginning to create their own family domains, enriching the land. They have adopted your image wholeheartedly, Anastasia — the marvellous image of the future for their family, the country and possibly the whole order of the Universe. They have understood all you have said and are building this marvellous future for themselves.

And I am trying to comprehend, too. I'm trying my best. I still don't completely understand what you mean to me. You taught me to write books, you bore me a son, you made me famous, you brought back my daughter's respect for me — you've done a lot! But that's not the main point. It's in something else, the main point. Perhaps it's lying hidden somewhere within.

You know, Anastasia, I have never spoken of my feelings for you, neither to you nor even to myself. In fact, I've never told any woman in my whole life that I love her.

I've never said that, not because I'm completely without feelings, but because these words have always seemed strange to me, even nonsensical. After all, if a person loves another, this love should be reflected in one's actions toward one's beloved. If words need to be spoken, that means there are no genuine, tangible actions. It's the actions, after all — not words — that are most important.

Anastasia stirred ever so slightly, took a deep breath, but did not waken. And I continued to talk with her, still speaking within myself.

Not once have I ever spoken to you about love, Anastasia. But if you asked me to fetch you a star from the sky, I would climb up to the top of the tallest tree, and pushing off from the uppermost branch, I'd take a leap in the direction of that star. If I happened to fall, I would catch myself on its branches, and climb up once more to the top, and again leap toward the star.

You've never asked me to fetch you a star from the sky. You only asked me to write books, and I am writing them. But my writing doesn't always come out too well. Sometimes I fall. But I'm not done with them yet, after all. I still haven't written my final book. I'll try to write it so you'll like it.

Anastasia's eyelashes fluttered, a gentle glow flushed across her cheeks, and she opened her eyes. I caught the tender gaze of her greyish-blue eyes... Oh, Lord, what a warmth those eyes always give off, especially when they're so close to me. Anastasia watched me without a word, but her eyes sparkled as though full of moisture.

"Good morning, Anastasia!" I said. "You probably haven't had a good long sleep like that before — you've always woken up before me."

"And a good morning to you, and a marvellous day, Vladimir," Anastasia responded quietly, almost in a whisper. "I should like to have just a wee bit more sleep."

"So you haven't had enough sleep yet?"

"I have, and a very good sleep at that. But my dream... I was having such a pleasant pre-dawn dream."

"What kind of dream? What was it about?"

"I dreamt you were talking with me. About a tall tree and a star, about falling down and climbing up again. The words were about the tree and the star, but it struck me as though they were really about love."

"Things can often seem pretty fuzzy in dreams. What connection could a tree possibly have with love?"

"Everything can have a connection, and great meaning too. It is the feelings that matter here, not the words. This day's dawn has brought me an extraordinary feeling. I shall go out to greet and embrace—"

"Who?"

"This marvellous day, which has offered me such an extraordinary gift."

Anastasia slowly rose to her feet, stepped a few paces away from the cave entrance and then... She did something she always did in the mornings — her unique exercise routine. There she was, flinging her arms out to the sides and a little bit upward. She gave a momentary glance up at the sky and then all at once spun round. Then she ran off and did an incredible somersault before spinning round again.

Lying on my sleeping bag by the cave entrance, I admired Anastasia's darts and lunges and thought: *Wow! A mature woman already, and look how quickly, beautifully and energetically she moves, just like a young gymnast! Fascinating, how she felt what I had in mind as I was talking to myself while she was sleeping! Maybe I really should own up to her?*

And I cried out:

"Anastasia, it wasn't simply a dream you were having."

She stopped her exercise routine at once and stood there in the middle of the glade. Then she deftly turned a couple of cartwheels in my direction and landed right beside me. She quickly sat down on the ground and joyfully enquired:

"Not simply a dream? And just how is it not 'simple'? Out with it! Tell me all the details!"

"Well, you see, *I* was thinking about that same tree. I was talking to myself about a star."

"And where, tell me, where did you get these words from? What produced them — these words?"

"Maybe feelings?"

Our conversation was interrupted by a cry from Anastasia's grandfather.

"Anastasia! Anastasia, listen to me right away! Do you read me?"

Anastasia jumped up, and I got up quickly, too.

CHAPTER TWO

Dominion over radiation

"Has Volodya been up to something unusual again?" Anastasia enquired of her grandfather, who had rushed over to us. And Grandfather, with a passing glance at me and a brief "Hello, Vladimir!", explained:

"He is down by the lakeshore. He dived down and brought up a stone from the bottom. Now he is standing there, clutching it in his hand. It is safe to assume that the stone is burning his hand, but he will not let it go. And I do not know what advice to give him."

Then Grandfather turned to me and barked:

"Your son's down there. You're his father. What are you standing here for?"

Not fully aware of what was going on, I ran down to the lake. Grandfather ran alongside me and explained:

"This stone is radioactive. It isn't big, but contains a good deal of energy — an energy similar to radiation."

"How did it happen to turn up at the bottom of the lake?"

"It's been lying there a long time. My father, even, knew about that stone. But nobody's been able to dive down to it."

"How did Volodya manage it? How did he know about it?"

"I trained him to do deep-water dives."

"What for?"

"He kept pestering me to show him, asking me again and again. You two don't seem to have the time to look after your own child's upbringing — you've been shoving the whole burden onto the shoulders of your elders."

"And who told him about the stone?"

"Now who would have told him, eh, apart from me? I told him."

"What for?"

"He wanted to know what stopped the lake from freezing over in winter."

As we approached the lake, I saw my son standing on the shore. His hair and shirt were all wet, but the water had already dripped off them, which told me he had been standing like that for some time.

Volodya stood with his arm stretched out in front of him, his fingers clenched into a fist, which he kept his eyes fixed on like a hawk. It was clear his hand was clutching that same sinister stone from the bottom of the lake. I took two steps in his direction. He quickly turned his head toward me and said:

"Don't come any closer, Papa."

And when I stopped, he added:

"Good health to your thoughts, Papa! But keep back just a little further. Maybe it would be better if you and Grandfather lay down on the ground. I shall be able to better concentrate that way."

Grandfather at once lay down on the ground, and without really knowing why, I followed suit. For some time we didn't say a word, just watching Volodya standing on the shore. Then a rather simple thought struck me, and I said:

"Volodya, couldn't you just toss it a little ways away?"

"Where away?" my son asked, not turning his head.

"Into the grass."

"I must not throw it into the grass. It could cause a lot of destruction. I feel I must not throw it away yet."

"So, does that mean you're going to keep standing there all day, or two days? What next? You're going to stand there a whole week? Or a month, even?"

"I am thinking about what to do, Papa. Let us keep quiet and give thought a chance to find the solution without being distracted."

Grandfather and I lay silently on the grass and looked at Volodya. And all at once I became aware of Anastasia approaching slowly — *too* slowly, under the circumstances — from the other end of the shore. When she got about five metres from Volodya's position, she sat down at the water's edge, as if nothing unusual were going on. She let her feet dangle in the water and stayed there that way for some time. Eventually she turned to our son and very calmly enquired:

"Is it burning your hand, son?"

"Yes, Mama," Volodya replied.

"What were you thinking about when you fetched the stone? And what are you thinking about right now?"

"The stone is giving off energy, similar to radiation. Grandfather was telling me about it. But Man[1] also gives off energy. I know that. And human energy is always stronger than any other — it cannot be dominated by any other. I brought up the stone and I am holding it. I am trying with all my might to repress its energy — to send it back inside the stone. I want to demonstrate that Man has dominion over any radiation."

"And are you succeeding in demonstrating the superiority of the energy coming from yourself?"

"Yes, Mama, I am succeeding. Only it is becoming increasingly hotter. It is burning my fingers and palm just a little."

"Why do you not throw it away?"

"I feel that I must not do that."

"Why?"

---

[1] *Man* — Throughout the Ringing Cedars Series, the word *Man* with a capital *M* is used to refer to a human being of either gender. For details on the word's usage and the important distinction between *Man* and *human being*, please see the Translator's Preface to Book 1.

"I feel it."

"Why?"

"It... It will explode, Mama. It will explode just as soon as I open my hand. There will be a big explosion."

"You are correct, it will explode. The stone is giving off the energy accumulated inside it. You used your own energy to repress its flow and direct it back inside. You used your thought to shape the nucleus within the stone, and *your* energy is now building up inside it, along with its own. It cannot go on accumulating indefinitely. It is already raging within the nucleus you formed with your own thoughts — it is getting hotter and the stone is burning your hand."

"I realise that, and that is why I am not letting go of my hold."

Outwardly Anastasia was the picture of calm. Her movements were slow and smooth, her speech was measured and with pauses. I could still feel, however, the extremely intense concentration of her thought — it must have been working faster than ever. She rose to her feet, gave what appeared to be a lethargic stretch, and said quietly:

"That means you realise, Volodya, that if you open your hand suddenly, there could be an explosion?"

"Yes, Mama."

"That means you have to release it gradually."

"How?"

"Just a tiny bit at first. First, ease up on your thumb and index finger to expose just a fraction of the stone. Picture in your mind right off how the energy you directed into the stone is emanating straight upward like a ray. And its own energy will begin to follow suit. Be careful: the ray must be directed only straight up."

Concentrating all his attention on his tightly clenched fist, Volodya gradually eased the pressure on his thumb and index finger. It was a sunny morning, but even in broad daylight one could see the ray emanating from the stone. A bird flying way up high fell into the ray and was immediately transformed into a puff of smoke. It looked as though a small cloud exploded in vapour when the ray passed through it. A few minutes later and the ray was scarcely noticeable.

"Oh, I have been sitting here with you too long!" said Anastasia. "I think I may go and make us some breakfast while you amuse yourselves here."

She took her time leaving. After going only a few steps, she staggered a bit, and then headed down to the water and washed her face. No doubt her outward calm had concealed an incredible inner tension. She had hid it so as not to frighten her son and interfere with his actions.

"How did you know exactly what I should do?" Volodya called out after the receding figure of Anastasia.

"How, indeed?" Grandfather echoed, mockingly. He had already got up from the ground and was feeling in much better spirits. "What do you mean, *how*? At school your Mama was a top-notch pupil in physics!" And he burst out in a loud guffaw.

Anastasia turned toward us and broke into laughter herself, explaining:

"I had not known about that before, son. But whatever happens, you always need to look for and find a solution. And not to let your thought be fettered by fear."

When the ray could no longer be seen at all, Volodya opened his hand completely. A small oblong stone was lying quietly on his palm. He stared at it for some time, muttering under his breath as he addressed the stone: "What is inside you is no match for Man!"

Then he once again closed his hand into a fist and dived straight into the water without taking off his shirt. It was a good three minutes before he resurfaced and headed back toward the shore.

"I was the one who taught him how to hold his breath that long," Grandfather commented.

After Volodya came out of the water, he jumped up and down to dry himself off, then headed over our way. I couldn't wait, but burst out:

"D'you have any idea what radiation is, son? I guess you don't. If you did, you wouldn't have gone and fetched that wretched stone. Can't you find yourself some other business to poke your nose into?"

"I know all about radiation, Papa. Grandfather told me about the disasters that have happened at your nuclear power plants, about your atomic weapons and the dangers now posed by the storage of nuclear waste."

"So, what's all the interest in this stone lying at the bottom of the lake? What about it?"

"Yes, indeed, what about it?" Grandfather joined the conversation. "*You* preach at him, Vladimir. I'm going to go have a little rest. It seems that lately your son's been making quite a few demands on me."

Grandfather started heading off, leaving me alone with my son.

And here he was, standing in front of me in his shirt, all dripping wet. He was evidently quite upset about the worry he had caused us all. I didn't feel like nagging him any further. I simply stood there without saying a word, not knowing how to begin. Volodya was the first to speak.

"You see, Papa, Grandfather told me that these nuclear waste facilities are extremely dangerous. According to probability theory, they can do irreparable harm to many countries and the people living in them. And to our whole planet, besides."

"They can, of course, but what's this got to do with you?"

"What this means is, if people think the problem is solved, but the danger still remains, it means they have not come up with the correct solution."

"So, what if it *is* incorrect — what does it matter?"

"Grandfather said that it is up to me to find the correct solution."

"So... have you found it?"

"I have now, Papa."

There he was, standing before me, my nine-year-old son, soaking wet and with an injured hand, but entirely confident in himself. And speaking in a calm and confident tone of voice about how to solve the problem of storing nuclear waste. An altogether peculiar situation! After all, he is no scientist, no nuclear physicist and doesn't even study in a regular school. Most peculiar! Here is this boy standing in his wet clothing on the shore of a taiga lake and discussing the safe storage of nuclear waste. Not counting on any kind of effective solution on his part, I asked, simply in the interests of keeping the conversation going:

"Well, what specific conclusions have you come to regarding this insoluble problem?"

"Out of all the possible variants, I think the most effective is deconcentration."

"I'm not sure what you mean — deconcentration of what?

"Of nuclear waste, Papa."

"How so?"

"I came to the realisation, Papa, that radiation in small doses is not at all dangerous. It is present in small quantities everywhere — in us, in plants, in the water and the clouds. But the real danger comes when too much is concentrated in one place. In the nuclear facilities Grandfather was telling me about, a whole lot of radioactive objects are concentrated together in one place."

"Well, everybody knows that. Radioactive waste is hauled to specially constructed storage facilities, which are carefully protected from terrorists. They've got specially trained personnel who ensure there are no violations of proper storage technology."

"Quite right, Papa. But the danger still exists. And a catastrophe is inevitable, caused by someone's specific thought imposing a wrong decision on people."

"You know, this problem, son, is being investigated in scientific institutes by highly qualified specialists. You're not a scholar, you haven't studied science, and so you're not capable of solving such an important question. It's modern science that ought to come up with an answer."

"But what has been the result, Papa? After all, it is precisely the inventions of modern science that have caused people to be subjected to great danger. Of course I do not study in school, and I do not know the science you are talking about, but..."

He fell silent and lowered his head.

"What does that 'but' of yours mean? Why did you stop, Volodya?"

"I have no desire, Papa, to be a pupil in that school or to study the science you have in mind."

"Why not?"

"Because, Papa, that kind of science is what leads to disasters."

"But there's no other kind of science."

"There is. 'Reality should be determined only through one's own self,' says Mama Anastasia. I understand what that means, and I am studying, or 'determining'. At the moment I do not know how to put it more specifically."

Wow! How sure he is of his convictions! I thought. Then I asked:

"And what is the probability of disaster, as you see it?"

"A hundred percent."

"You're certain of that?"

"According to probability theory and the absence of any counteraction to destructive thought, a disaster is inevitable. The construction of large nuclear storage facilities can be compared to the construction of huge bombs."

"And am I to guess that your thought has begun counter-acting this destructive element?"

"Yes, I have launched my thought into space. And it will triumph."

"Specifically, what solution has your thought come up with regarding the problem of the safe storage of nuclear waste?"

"All nuclear waste concentrated in large facilities needs to be deconcentrated — that is my thought."

"Deconcentration — does that mean dividing it into frag-ments a hundred thousandth or a multi-millionth in size?"

"That is right, Papa."

"A simple solution. But the big question remains: where to store these tiny fragments?"

"On kin's domains, Papa."

For a moment the shock of this incredible statement com-pletely overwhelmed me — I didn't know what to say. Then I practically shouted:

"Nonsense! That's utter nonsense you've thought up, Volodya."

After I'd thought about it a little more, I said in a calmer voice:

"Of course, if nuclear fragments are deconcentrated and spread among various places, a global catastrophe can be averted. But this will also put millions of families who have decided to live on these domains in danger. After all, every-body wants to live in a place that's environmentally clean."

"Yes, Papa, everybody wants to live in an environmentally clean place. But there are hardly any such places remaining on the Earth today."

"And here in the taiga, isn't this environmentally clean ei-ther?"

"The environment here is relatively clean. But it is not ideal, not pristine. There are no ideal spots left, anywhere. Clouds can bring their acid rain here too, from a variety of places. The grass and trees and bushes are coping with it for the time be-ing, but the filthy places are becoming only filthier with each passing day. And the number of such places keeps growing with each passing day. That is why it is essential right now not to walk away from this filthiness, but attack it. 'We need to create clean places ourselves' — that is what Mama says.

"From all the possible variants my thought selected just one. It could not come up with any other. My thought tells me it is safer to deconcentrate and tame the waste one frag-ment at a time, and derive a benefit for life on our planet by storing a tiny fragment on one's domain."

"But where on the domain? In a larder? In a safe? Store this radioactive capsule in an underground cellar? Has your thought given you any hint of this yet?"

"The capsule should be buried underground no less than nine metres deep."

I spent some time thinking about my son's proposal, which had indeed seemed incredible at first, but the more I thought about it, the more inclined I became to accept that there was some grain of reason in what he said. At the very least, his proposal for nuclear waste storage would be entirely suffi-cient to avert a large-scale catastrophe. As to pollution on the given domain, that was something that could indeed be avoided, and there might even be a plus side. Perhaps scien-tists could come up with something like a mini-reactor — or something similar.

And then, all at once a thought dawned on me. Wow! Here was another reason for the need to deconcentrate the storage of radioactive waste. *Money!*

Huge sums are being doled out by foreign governments for the storage of such waste. It is these funds that pay for constructing the facilities, maintaining service personnel and whole security control systems. And a part of this money inevitably disappears into the unknown. Why not pay it, instead, to every domain where radioactive waste capsules are stored? Fantastic! Not only would 'safe contamination' be guaranteed, but people would earn money besides.

At the present time nobody can guarantee security from contamination even for those living far away from the storage facilities. Think what happened at Chernobyl[2] — the contamination affected not just parts of Ukrainian territory, but of Russia and Belarus as well. Clouds can carry the pollution for hundreds and even thousands of kilometres.

So, even though it is still at the conceptual stage and the details need fleshing out, my son's proposal deserves serious consideration — not just on the part of the academic world, but from governments, and especially the public.

I was walking along the lakeshore, immersed in my thoughts, and had quite forgot about my son. He was still standing at the same spot, silently watching me. His upbringing forbade him from being the first to reinitiate our conversation. To interrupt the thought of a Man in contemplation was unthinkable.

I decided to change the subject.

"So, you spend your time thinking about different problems, Volodya. Don't you have any duties to carry out? Have you been assigned any work to perform?"

"Work?... Assigned?... I always do what I feel like doing. Work? What do you mean by the word *work*, Papa?"

"Well, work is when you carry out some kind of task, and people pay you money for it. Or when you do something that's going to benefit your whole family. Take me, for

---

[2]*Chernobyl* — a town in northern Ukraine with a nuclear-power generating station. In April 1986 an accident at Reactor N° 4 caused one of Europe's worst environmental disasters, spreading dangerous radiation over a huge land area. As a result of the accident, the population of Chernobyl (13,000 people) and nearby Pripiat' (49,000) was evacuated, and these towns, as well as the larger surrounding area, are now uninhabited.

example — when I was your age, my parents assigned me to look after our bunny-rabbits. And that's what I did. I would collect grass for them, feed them, clean their cages... And the rabbits brought our family a bit of income."

After hearing me out, Volodya suddenly said with some excitement:

"Papa, I shall tell you about one particular duty which I assigned to myself — a very enjoyable duty. Only you'll have to judge whether it can be called *work* or not."

"Tell me about it."

"Then let's go. I have a specific place I want to show you."

CHAPTER THREE

"Goosey, goosey, ga-ga-ga"[1] *or*
The superknowledge we are losing

We started heading off from the lake, Volodya leading the way. He had changed somehow. His analytical and concentrated mood had given way to one of joyfulness and excitement. Sometimes he would do a pirouette as he walked along, or a little leap into the air, as he explained to me:

"I never looked after bunny-rabbits, Papa. I did something else. I am not sure what to call it — *gave birth?* That will not do. *Created?* Not really... Ah, now I remember. I think in your civilisation it is called *sitting on eggs.* So, I sat on some eggs."

"What d'you mean, you sat on some eggs? That's a mother hen's job, or some other kind of bird's."

"Yes, I know. But in my case I had to sit on them myself."

"What for? Tell me everything, in the proper order."

"All right, in the proper order. Well, it happened in this order:

"I asked Grandfather to find me some eggs laid by wild ducks and wild geese. At first Grandfather grumbled a bit, but three days later he brought me four large goose eggs, along with five duck eggs, which were smaller.

"Next in order, I dug a little hole in the ground, and put some deer manure in the bottom along with grass stalks, and then I

---

[1]*Goosey, goosey, ga-ga-ga* — the first line of a popular Russian folk song. The song accompanies a children's game in which a group of children (representing a flock of geese) are fleeing home from their feeding grounds while another child (as a wolf) tries to catch them.

. covered them over with dried grass, and then on top of this I placed the two sets of eggs Grandfather had brought me."

"What was the manure for?"

"For warmth. Eggs need warmth to hatch. And they need warmth from above, too. Sometimes I lay down on the ground myself, covering the hole with my stomach. When it was cold or rainy, I assigned this task to the bear."

"How did the bear keep from crushing the eggs?"

"You see, even though the bear is big, the hole containing the eggs is pretty small. He lay on top of the hole, and the eggs were at the bottom. Sometimes I would have the she-wolf guard the eggs, at other times I would sleep on the ground nearby myself, until they started to hatch. It was so wonderful to watch them hatching. Not all of them made it, though. From the nine eggs I started with, were born two goslings and three ducklings. I fed them grass seed and crushed nuts and gave them water to drink. Whenever I fed them, I would invite various creatures living on our territory to watch."

"What for?"

"To show them how I cared for the little chicks, to help them understand that they should not touch them, but that they should protect them instead. I would also sleep beside the hole where the goslings and ducklings were born, except on cold or rainy nights when I had the bear take over for me. The chicks nestled in his warm coat, which made it very nice for them.

"Next, if I am to proceed in the proper order: I put up stakes around the hole with which I made a wicker fence from branches, and put branches above the nest as well. As the goslings and ducklings grew and learnt to climb out of their hole, I would walk around their nest and make short whistling sounds: *tsu-tsu-tsu.* Upon hearing this, they would immediately climb out and run after me. They tried running after the bear, but I trained them out of it. The bear can travel quite a distance, and the birds might not make it in one piece.

"But nothing happened to them. They grew up, feathers appeared, and they learnt to fly. I would toss them up in the air to help them along. Then they began flying off on their own, but always returned to their nest.

"When autumn came and a whole lot of birds started gathering in flocks to fly south, my grown-up ducks attached themselves to a whole flock of ducks, and my geese joined a flock of geese, and they all flew off to warmer climes.

"But I guessed — I was almost certain — that they would return in the spring. And they did. Oh, how fantastic that was, Papa! They came back, and I heard their delightful cry: *ga-ga-ga*. I ran over to their nest and began calling: *tsu-tsu-tsu*. I fed them grass seed and some nut kernels which I had ground up beforehand. They took the feed right out of my hands. I was so happy, and all the creatures around heard the cry and came running oh so happily...

"Look, Papa, here we are! Look!"

There in a secluded spot between two currant bushes I saw the nest my son had fashioned. But there was no wildlife to be seen anywhere around.

"You say they've come back, but there aren't any birds here."

"Not at the moment. They have flown off somewhere to have a stroll or look for food. That is why they are not here right now, but look, Papa!"

As Volodya pushed the branches aside to widen the opening, I caught a glimpse of three nest holes. In one of them lay five small-sized eggs, probably, duck eggs. In the other, just one, slightly larger — a goose egg.

"Wow! That means they *have* come back. And they're laying eggs. Only just a few."

"Yes!" Volodya exclaimed in excitement. "They have come back and are laying eggs. They could lay more if I took some of the eggs out of the nest and fed the mothers more often."

I looked at my son's happy face, but could not fully comprehend the reason for his joyful excitement. I asked him:

"What are you so fantastically happy about, Volodya? I know none of you — either you or your Mama or your grandfather — eat eggs. Which means that your actions cannot be called 'work' or a 'job', since there's no practical benefit from it."

"You think so? But remember, other people eat bird's eggs. Mama says it is all right to use anything the animals themselves give to Man. Especially for people who are not accustomed to a vegetarian diet."

"What have other people got to do with your activities here?"

"I have decided that something needs to be done so that people living on their domains can be free from the burden of so many household tasks. Or almost free. So that they can have time to think and reflect. This is possible — if you understand God's intent in creating our world. I find delight in the science of getting to know His thoughts. It is certainly the grandest science of all, and it is something that must be known.

"We need to learn, for example, why He made the birds fly south in the autumn, but they do not stay in those warmer climes, but come back in the spring. I have thought a lot about this, and have guessed that He did this so that Man would not be burdened during the wintertime. In winter birds cannot find food for themselves, and they fly away. But they do not stay in the south, but come back — they want to be useful to Man. This is God's intent. There is much for Man to learn from what our Creator has conceived."

"What you're suggesting, then, Volodya, is that ducks and geese can live in every domain, lay their eggs, feed themselves, and then fly off in the autumn and come back in the spring?"

"Yes, quite right. After all, it worked with me."

"Yes, I see — it really did work with you. But there's just one concern I have... It will probably upset you to hear this, but still, I have to tell you the truth. Just so you don't go looking ridiculous with your proposal."

"Tell me the truth, Papa."

"You see, there's this science we call economics. Economists are trying to figure out what is the best way of handling the production of various goods — in this case, eggs. In our world a lot of chicken farms have been set up, where a whole bunch of chickens are kept in one place. They lay their eggs, and afterward these eggs are shipped off to grocery stores. People can go to these stores and easily purchase as many eggs as they need. It's all worked out to ensure the least expenditure of labour and time on a per-unit basis."

"What does 'expenditure of labour' mean, Papa?"

"It refers to the quantity of time and resources spent on the production of a single egg. You have to carefully work out what's going to be the most efficient method of production, and that will be the best method."

"Fine, I shall try to work it out, Papa."

"When you work out the whole thing, you'll understand. But to figure it out you'll need expense statistics. I'll try to get them from some economist."

"But I can calculate everything right now, Papa."

Volodya gave a bit of a frown, evidently concentrating, and after a minute announced:

"*Minus two to infinity.*"

"What kind of a formula is that? What does it refer to?"

"The efficiency of the Divine economy is expressed in an infinite series of numbers. Even starting from zero, modern scientific economics is already two points down."

"You've got a pretty strange method of calculation there. I can't fathom it. Can you explain how you arrived at that figure?"

"I set the benchmark for our current case at zero. All the expenses involved in a chicken factory — its construction, maintenance and delivery of eggs to stores are summed up in the figure of minus one."

"What d'you mean, 'minus one'? These expenses should be expressed in roubles and kopeks."[2]

"Monetary units are relative and will always vary, and so they are not significant in this methodology. They all need to be lumped together under the arbitrary value of 'minus one'. Whatever expenses there are, in terms of a zero benchmark, they can be expressed as 'minus one'."

"And where did you get the second minus figure?"

"That is *quality*. It cannot be very good. The unnatural maintenance conditions and the lack of variety in feed cannot help but lower the quality of the eggs, and this gives rise to another value of minus one. So we get 'minus two' altogether."

"Okay, let's say you're right. But in your case, too, there are huge expenditures of time. Here, tell me, Volodya, how much time did you spend, as you put it, 'sitting on' the eggs, and then feeding the ducklings and goslings, and watching out for them?"

"Ninety days and nights."

"So, ninety times twenty-four hours. And all that in aid of producing no more than a few dozen eggs — and that only at the end of a year! For people living in their domains, it would be much more efficient to buy some little chicks at a market or hatch them over the winter with the help of an electric incubator, and in four or five months they'll start laying. In the

---

[2]*kopek* (Russian: *kopeika*) — a coin worth 1/100 of a rouble. It is derived from the Russian word for 'spear' (*kop'ë*, pronounced *kap-YO*), in reference to a warrior piercing a dragon with his spear — a scene depicted on early Russian coins. The word 'rouble' itself is derived from the verb *rubit'* ('cut with an axe') — early coins represented a silver band cut in rectangular pieces.

second year, before winter sets in, they're generally slaugh-
tered, since their laying capacity goes down by the third year.
So they kill them and start raising a new batch. That's technology for you."

"That is the technology of never-ending burdens, Papa.
You have to feed the chickens every day, store up food for the
winter, and every other year raise a new batch of chickens."

"Sure, you feed them and raise new ones, but thanks to
modern technology it isn't nearly as time-consuming as your
alternative."

"But those ninety days will launch a programme that will
last forever. Once they come back, the migratory birds will
raise their young all by themselves, they will teach them how
to get along with human beings and come back to their home-
land. And they will go on doing this for thousands of years.
In launching a programme like this, Man is passing it on to
future generations of his family. He is giving back to them a
little particle of the Divine economy. A hundred years from
now an expenditure of ninety days in calculating the cost of
producing a single egg, will count as minutes, and continue to
diminish with each passing year."

"But still, there are expenses, and you haven't taken these
into account."

"These expenses are offset by a powerful counterweight,
which is no less significant than what is produced by the
birds."

"What counterweight?"

"When birds once again fly from faraway lands back to
their native woods and fields, people are delighted to see
them. Thanks to their joyful and beneficial energy, many people's diseases are eliminated. But this energy is ninety times
stronger when they do not merely fly back from the south,
but come directly to you and start greeting the Man living on
that domain with their happy cries and refrains of exultation.

Their singing brings joy and strength not only to Man but to the whole Space around him."

Volodya spoke with confidence and inspiration. It would have seemed foolish to continue arguing with him. I pretended to be absorbed in contemplation or to be figuring out something in my mind. I felt a little put out that there was nothing I could teach my son or even offer him a few hints on.

And what kind of upbringing or education do we have here anyway? Here is my son standing right in front of me, and yet he seems like a child from another planet or another civilisation.

He has a different concept of life, a different philosophy and speed of thought. He can do instantaneous calculations. And it is clear, as I have been made aware, that even if I spent a year on computer calculations, whatever he comes up with would still be more accurate. It's as though everything inside him were turned upside-down. Or perhaps it might be more accurate to ask: *To what degree have we perverted our own lives — our concepts and meaning of life?* All our disasters have arisen from these perversions.

No doubt this is all true, but still... I'm so anxious to find some way of being useful to my son. But how? With no expectations left, I asked him quietly and offhandedly:

"I'll give some thought to those economics of yours. Maybe you're right... But tell me, son: you've been playing with different tasks here, working them out. Have you ever had a really *serious* problem to meet?"

Volodya sighed deeply and, it seemed, rather woefully. After a brief pause he replied:

"Yes, Papa, I do have a big problem. And only you can help me solve it."

Volodya was sad, while I, on the other hand, was delighted to find something at last where he required my help.

"And what does it involve, this big problem of yours?"

A big problem

"Remember, Papa, when I told you last time you were here that I was preparing to go off into your world when I grew up?"[3]

"Yes, I remember. You said you would come into our world and find yourself a Universe Girl to make her happy. You'd build a kin's domain with her, and raise children together. I remember your telling me. So, you haven't abandoned your project?"

"Not at all. And I often think of the future, about that girl and the domain. I can picture in detail how she and I will live there together. And how you and Mama will come visit and see how the dream which that girl and I co-created together is being turned into reality."

"Well, then, what's your problem? Are you afraid you might not find your girl?"

"That is not the problem. I shall look for this girl and find her. Come, I shall show you another little glade. And you will see it all for yourself— you will sense what the problem is."

Volodya and I arrived at a small glade located right next door to Anastasia's. When we reached the middle of the glade, we stopped, and Volodya invited me to sit down on the ground. Then, cupping his hands around his mouth, he gave out a loud and extended cry: *A-a-a-a!* First he cried out in one direction, then another and yet another. In just two or three

---

[3]See Book 6, Chapter 2: "Conversation with my son", especially the section "I shall make a Universe Girl happy".

minutes there began a rustling in the treetops all around the glade, and a whole lot of squirrels could be seen leaping from branch to branch, gathering together on a single cedar tree. Some of them simply sat down on one of the branches and stared in our direction, while others — apparently the more restless ones — continued hopping from one branch to another.

A few minutes later and out of the bushes came running three wolves. They sat down at the edge of the glade and also began looking our way.

A sable came along and took up a position about three metres from the wolves. Then two goats appeared. They didn't sit down, but stood at the edge of the glade, their eyes fixed on us. Soon afterward came a deer. The last to arrive was a huge bear, noisily making his way through the bushes. He too sat down at the edge of the glade, panting all the while, saliva dripping from his tongue. He had probably been a long ways off and had had to run for some distance.

All this time Volodya stood behind my back, with his hands on my shoulders. Then he took a few paces back from me and picked some herbs. Coming back to me, he said:

"Open your mouth, Papa, and I shall give you some herbs to eat. This is so they can see that I am feeding you from my hand, and will not be upset at the sight of a stranger."

I took the proffered herbs in my mouth and began to chew. Volodya sat down beside me, put his head up against my chest and said:

"Stroke my hair, Papa, so that they will fully calm down."

I began stroking his light-brown hair with delight. Then he sat down beside me and began to explain.

"I realised, Papa, that God created the whole world as a cradle for His son, Man. The plants, the air, the water and clouds — everything has been created for Man. And the creatures stand ready to serve Man with great delight. But we have forgotten, and now it is important to understand what services the creatures can perform, what their purpose and destiny is. Even today a lot of people are aware that a dog can guard the house, find lost objects, and aid in keeping one's home safe from intruders. A cat, of course, can catch the mice that raid the larder. A horse is transportation. But all the other creatures have a specific feature and designation, too, which should be understood. I have tried the best I could to determine the function of all that you see here.

"Now they are sitting there and awaiting my command. This is the third year now I have been working with them to understand their purpose. Take, for example, the bear. Because of his big and powerful paws, he can dig an underground cellar, put supplies in it to save for the winter and dig them up again in the spring. He knows how to bring honey from a tree hollow."

"Yes, I know, Volodya. Anastasia told me that at one time people used bears as household help."

"Mama told me that, too. But look what I have taught the bear to do."

Volodya rose to his feet and stretched out his right arm in the bear's direction. The bear drew himself up on his haunches, and even seemed to stop breathing. When Volodya clapped his hand against his thigh, the huge bear took several giant strides and lay down at the boy's feet. Volodya squatted down beside the beast's enormous head, gave it a slap and began scratching behind the creature's ear. The bear purred with pleasure. When Volodya got up, the bear did the same, watching the boy's every move.

Volodya went over to the edge of the glade, where he found a dry branch, and stuck it into the ground about ten metres from where I was sitting. Then he returned to the edge and approached a small cedar tree about a metre high. He touched it and clapped his hands twice. Right off, the bear ran over to the cedar and sniffed it. And then an incredible thing started to happen.

My son sat down beside me on the grass and the two of us began watching as the scene unfolded before our eyes.

The bear spent some time sniffing the little cedar. First he would walk away from it, as though measuring something, then he would run over to the spot where Volodya's dry branch was sticking up. And all around the branch he suddenly began scraping away the earth with his front paws.

Working furiously with his paws and their powerful claws, in the space of a few minutes he had dug a hole approximately 80 cm in diameter and about half a metre deep. He stopped to admire his handiwork, and even stuck his head into the pit, probably to sniff it.

After that the bear ran over to the cedar Volodya had indicated, and began to dig out the earth around it. When he had dug what amounted to a circular trench, the bear sat down on his hind paws next to the cedar, dug his front paws into the trench and pulled the little tree out of the ground, along with a sizeable clump of earth. Rising on his hind legs, he held the clump between his front paws and headed over to the hole he had dug earlier. He carefully sat down and lowered the clump with the cedar into the hole. It turned out the hole was about 15 cm larger than required. The bear backed off to take a look at his handiwork. Once more he pulled out the cedar and set it to one side, while he filled in the hole just a little more, before replanting the cedar. Now everything was just right.

The bear backed away to once more inspect his accomplishment. This time he was apparently satisfied, as he went back to the cedar he had planted and began filling in the crevice around the clump from which the tree was growing. He used his paw to scoop up the earth, stuff it into the crevice and then pack it down around the newly replanted tree.

It was quite a fascinating scene, but I had earlier witnessed how the squirrels brought dried mushrooms and nuts for Anastasia,[4] or how the wolves played with Anastasia and protected her from wild dogs.[5]

Not only that, but a lot of people can observe all sorts of tricks with various animals just by attending a circus performance. My own dog Kedra[6] also takes delight in carrying out a range of commands.

What I witnessed in the taiga glade also bore outward similarities to a circus performance, except that it didn't take place in an arena surrounded by a high net, but in natural surroundings. And the performers were not circus animals living in confined cages, but free — or 'wild', as we call them — dwellers in the taiga. They might well have seemed wild to us, but to my son they were simply friends and helpers. Just like our household pets and farm animals.

However, I must point out one mysterious and incredible distinction in particular: the loyalty of household pets and farm animals can be explained by the fact that Man gives them food and drink and provides shelter. People who go see animal acts at circuses may also notice that after each successful trick the tamer rewards the lion or tiger, giving them some kind of treat or trifle he keeps on his belt or in his pocket just for that purpose.

Circus animals which spend years confined in cages have no opportunity to hunt for their own food. They are fully dependent on Man. By contrast, the creatures here in the taiga are absolutely free and fully capable of finding food and shelter on their own. Yet still they come — not just come, but

---

[4]See, for example, Book 1, Chapter 6: "Anastasia's morning".

[5]See, for example, Book 3, Chapter 12: "Man-made mutants".

[6]*Kedra* — a name derived from *kedr* (the Russian word for 'cedar' or 'Siberian pine').

make an enthusiastic dash to respond to Man's call and carry out his commands. They carry them out with considerable desire and even servility. Why? What do they get in return? Volodya gave no food to the bear. But still, the bear's joy was many times more clearly evident than that shown by the circus animals upon receiving their treat.

The bear that transplanted the little tree on Volodya's command stood there shifting from paw to paw, his eyes fixed on the boy, as though he wanted to repeat the action or perform some other task. It is strange how this huge taiga bear really wants to keep on doing something for Man, and for a child at that.

Volodya was not about to set the bear any new task. He gestured the bear to come over, grasped the fur on the bear's muzzle with both hands, ruffled it a bit, then petted the muzzle and said:

"You're a super helper — not like the goats."

The bear purred with delight. This threatening creature sounded as though it was at the very pinnacle of bliss.

Anastasia has said:

"Such beneficial energy can flow from Man as has never before been seen. Every living creature on the Earth needs this energy just as it needs air, sunshine and water. And even sunlight is but a reflection of the great energy emanating from Man."

Our sciences have discovered a multitude of diverse energies and even brought about the artificial generation of electrical energy. They have split the atom and manufactured bombs. But how far (and in what direction) have our sciences advanced in studying the more significant and important question as to the energy emanating from Man himself? Is there any tendency toward studying this energy at all, including its mysterious capabilities? Or studying Man's abilities in general, and his function in both our world and the Universe?

Perhaps someone is trying by whatever means available to hinder Man from knowing himself. And I mean actual hindering.

It cannot be, it cannot possibly be Man's destiny to spend years sitting in a casino or at a bar for a shot of vodka, or drudging away at a cash register in some store or at a manager's desk in some office. And even a supermodel, or a president, or a pop-star — none of them come even close to Man's most important purpose.

And yet it is these very professions of our modern age, along with making money, that some enigmatic 'entity' is promoting today as the most important thing in Man's life. It's what we see in a good many of our films and TV shows, which concentrate on everything except the meaning of life. All they do is turn Man into a banana-head.

Isn't that the reason wars are happening all over the place? And the Earth is becoming more and more polluted? And people lose their sense of direction, they see no purpose in living, and so they take to vodka and drugs.

Who is supposed to stop all this rot that is taking place with our Earth? *Science?* But science isn't saying anything. *Religion?* Which religion? Where are the results? Maybe everyone needs to ponder this for themselves? Ponder it! For themselves!

To ponder, one must first think. But where? When? Our lives have become one giant bustle from morning 'til night.

Every single attempt that has ever been made to ponder the meaning of life has been suddenly aborted. Selling magazines featuring half-naked sensuous bodies — oh, sure! Savouring sexual perversion — oh, sure! Showing and telling about the beastly antics of pervert-maniacs — oh, sure! Writing and talking about prostitutes in the media — oh, sure!

But there is less and less talk about the meaning of Man's life and Man's purpose — it's becoming more and more a taboo topic.

I glanced up from my contemplations to look at my son. He was sitting on the grass beside me, watching me intently. I thought he might have something more he wanted to show me. I asked him:

"And what was it you were saying to the bear about *goats*, Volodya?"

"I cannot, for the life of me, Papa, determine what their purpose is."

"What's there to determine? Everyone knows what goats are for — to give milk to Man."

"Yes, milk, of course. But perhaps there is something more they can be taught."

"What more could they possibly...? Why bother looking for something else?"

"I have been watching them. Goats are capable of stripping bark off trees and stumps. And they can bite off branches from bushes. If you let them into a domain, they could cause harm to the plants. To stop that from happening, I am trying to teach them to trim the hedges around the domains."

"Trim?"

"Yes, Papa, trim. After all, people trim hedges to make them more beautiful — either in a straight line or in different shapes. Grandfather told me you call it landscape design, or topiary art. But the goats do not seem to have any concept of what I want them to do."

"And how are you teaching them?"

"I shall show you."

Volodya reached for a rope made of nettle fibres woven together, about three metres long. He fastened one end to a small tree and stretched the rope through a clump of bushes. Then, gesturing the two little goats to approach, he gave each of them a pat. He touched the bushes with his hand and even snapped off a small branch himself with his teeth. He said

something to the goats, and they set about vigorously gnaw-
ing off the bushy branches. Each time they neared the rope
border, Volodya would give several tugs on the rope and make
some disapproving sounds. The goats would stop for a time,
holding their snouts up and looking enquiringly at the boy,
but then go back to biting off the branches, paying no attention to the rope.

"You see, Papa, it is not working. They do not realise they
are supposed to trim the bushes in an even line."

"Yes, I see. Is that the problem you were talking about?"

"That is not the main problem, Papa. It is something
else."

"Then what?"

"You noticed, Papa, how happily the different creatures
came running to my call?"

"Yes, I did."

"I have been working with them for several years now, and
they have become accustomed to communicating with me,
but only with me. They look forward to this interchange,
they want to be petted. But once I go off into your world,
they will miss me. They will miss not having a Man ever come
to see them again, or call them and give them something to
do. I feel that the communication with Man and serving Man
has become the most significant focus in their life."

"Couldn't they communicate with Anastasia?"

"Mama has her own circle, her own creatures she is friends
with. Besides, she is very busy and does not have time for all
of them.

"But, you see, *these*..." — and here once again Volodya
pointed to the creatures still sitting around the edge of the
glade — these I chose myself, and I am the only one who has
been working with them these past few years.

"Three months ago I asked Grandfather to be present with
me at all our training sessions. Grandfather muttered, but he

was always there beside me. But recently he told me he would be unable to replace me."

"Why?"

"He said he did not have the same interest as I had in animal-training. And once again he began to mutter that I should not have spent so much time with the animals individually. And that I should not have given them so much petting. And he reminded me that these creatures look upon me not only as their leader, but as their child, too, since the older among them saw me when I was a baby and even nursed me. You see, I made some kind of mistake, and now I must definitely correct it. Only now I am no longer able to correct it all on my own."

I looked at the creatures still sitting at the edge of the glade. They gave every indication that they were waiting for Volodya to give them some sort of instructions or to do something with them. I imagined how they would miss him if he were to go away. The same way my dog Kedra misses me when I have to leave my home in the country for days or weeks at a time. She has a warm little doghouse and I don't keep her chained up — she's free to roam the fields or the forest or the village. And I have a neighbour who feeds her every day. He makes *kasha*[7] for her, and gives her bones to chew on. But my neighbour tells me:

"She misses you, Vladimir Nikolaevich. She'll often sit by the gate and gaze down the road you come home on. And sometimes she'll whimper."

And whenever I arrive, Kedra rushes headlong to greet me, rubs against my legs, and sometimes she's so enthusiastic she'll jump right up and try to lick my face, soiling my clothes

---

[7]*kasha* — a traditional Russian and Eastern European porridge made with wheat, buckwheat and other grains.

with her dirty paws. And there's no way I can train her to be not quite so ebullient in expressing her emotions.

But these creatures in the glade... All the time we talked they sat there quietly watching us, looking the picture of composure. What do they want? After all, nobody is making them sit that way or wait on some kind of command from Man.

My God... A thought all at once bubbled up with absolute clarity and struck my heart. It was much more than just about these creatures sitting in a taiga glade — it was the realisation that all the creatures on the Earth have a specific purpose and await contact with the highest being on the planet, namely, Man. They have been created to help Man fulfil his supreme mission. Like all life on the planet, they were created by God to help Man realise his grand destiny... But Man...

I looked at the creatures in the glade and began to realise that my son really did have a serious problem on his hands: he could not simply abandon these creatures. Nor could he bring himself to give up his dream about the girl he would be setting up a domain with.

"Yes, Volodya, that really is a problem," I told my son. "Doesn't look as though there's any solution. Not one we can find."

"There *is* a solution, Papa, but it does not depend on me."

"On whom, then?"

"*You* are the only one who can solve this problem, Papa."

"Me? And just how am I supposed to do that? There's nothing *I* can do here, son."

There is a solution

"I think, Papa, that you will be able to help me if you really want to," said Volodya quietly.

"You think so? But, you see, I have no idea what to do. *You* may think so, but I have no idea."

I was still sitting on the grass, while Volodya stood in front of me, looking me in the eye with some kind of an imploring gaze, his lips whispering something inaudible. I could tell by his lips that he was saying one particular word over and over again. Then, without taking his eyes away, he said it distinctly:

"*Sis-ter.* I earnestly beg of you, Papa, to bear me a sister, together with Mama. I shall nurse her and raise her myself. They will help me. We shall not distract you and Mama from your activities. I shall teach her, when she grows a little. I shall tell her about everything. She will remain here with my creatures and my Space.

"Bear me a sister, together with Mama. Unless, of course, you are ill... or are too tired. That is, of course, if you can. Grandfather told me that men in your world often get ill and grow older faster because of the way of life there, the air not fit to breathe and the foul water. You are a little past fifty years old, Papa. But if you are tired, Papa... If your strength is pretty much exhausted... Then spend three days with me. Just three days. I have everything all prepared, and a great deal of strength will be restored to you."

My son was excited, and I interrupted him.

"Wait, Volodya, calm down. Of course I'm a little tired. But I think I'll have enough strength. That's not the point. In principle I have nothing against giving you a sister, but when it comes to bearing children, a desire on the part of *both* parents is required."

"I am sure of it, Papa. I know for certain that Mama will not refuse. If you agree, let us not waste any time, but begin right now to prepare for the birth of my sister. I have been studying up on it. Grandfather has helped me a great deal. I have made calculations and have everything prepared. Stay with me three days and three nights, and do not go off anywhere, and do not get distracted by anything, Papa. Your energy and strength will increase."

"What makes you think I don't have enough energy or strength, Volodya?"

"I think you have enough, but you shall have more."

"Okay, I shall spend all three days with you alone, but we must go and let Mama know."

"I shall explain everything to her myself, Papa. I shall tell her we have a common project. She will not go into specifics and will not object."

"Well, all right, then, let's get started."

I even began to wonder what my son had prepared that would restore a great deal of strength and energy to Man after only three days. And I shall say right off that the procedures he prepared may seem rather strange, but the sensation resulting from them on the third day defies explanation in words or writing.

It wouldn't be appropriate, either, to say that a Man becomes ten or twenty years younger, though he may indeed look as much as five years younger. But on the *inside...* Somehow everything inside me seemed to be working differently. Not only did I have new strength, but the world around me seemed just a bit different.

CHAPTER FOUR

Rejuvenation

First ordeal

No sooner had I agreed to follow through with the procedures thought up by my son than he signalled the assembled creatures to *go away*. He grasped hold of my hand, and we ran down to the lake. Volodya stopped several times along the way to pick herbs in various places, which he softened and rolled into a ball. When the ball was ready, he instructed me to eat it, which I did. And in just a few minutes I noticed a heavy drip of snot exuding from my nose and I began to vomit. It seemed that all my stomach juices had been pumped out. I was unable to speak for all the vomiting, while Volodya explained:

"That is good, Papa. Do not be afraid. It is good for all that useless stuff to come out of you. Only a pure state will remain. This is what they do in cases of poisoning."

I was physically unable to offer any kind of answer, but thought to myself: *That's true: poisoning victims drink tablets which produce nausea and vomiting. There are laxatives, of course — castor oil, for example. But what do I need this ordeal for? I haven't been poisoned.*

As though he had tuned in to my question, Volodya explained:

"You, of course, have not been poisoned, Papa, but the food you have been consuming is right on the verge of having a poisoning effect. Just let go of everything filthy inside you."

After the vomiting and the discharge of the phlegm from my nose, along with a copious flow of tears from my eyes,

I began having a series of soft bowel movements, and five times I ended up running into the bushes for a lengthy period. The whole procedure lasted two to three hours. Then came relief.

"Now do you feel better, Papa? Better than before? Eh?"

"Yes," I affirmed.

Second ordeal

Volodya once again took hold of my hand and off we ran. When we reached the shore of the lake, he instructed me to wash myself and swim around a bit. Upon coming out of the water, I noticed him extracting a clay jar from a hole in the ground, about a litre and a half in size.

"Now, Papa, you need to drink this water. It is called *dead water* — because it contains very few microbes. This water should not be drunk if the air is polluted. But we have pure air here, so it is all right to drink dead water. It will rinse your insides and cleanse them, and wash out a lot of microbes and bacteria from your body. Drink as much as you can, Papa. When you have drunk up this whole jar, I shall give you another, and when you have finished that I shall give you a third jar, containing living water. And all the microbes and bacteria you need will be restored in a balance that is just right for you."

I should point out right off that Volodya and his family consider dead water to be that found at great depths below the Earth's surface and containing a minimum of bacteria. I believe our mineral water in bottles is precisely what they call dead water. In any case, I think *all* of our drinking water is dead water, and that is why our children suffer from disbacteriosis, especially newborns.

Living water, on the other hand, they consider to be surface water from pure streams or bodies of water, a few of which have indeed been preserved in the depths of the Siberian taiga.

There's something I wish to emphasise here. Grandfather later explained to me that spring water is not considered living water when you drink it right out of the spring. To be considered 'living water', it must first be kept for three hours or so in a wooden or clay vessel with a wide neck.

"Living water needs to absorb sunlight," he said. "With the aid of sunlight, organisms are generated which are indispensable to human life. You call them microbes and bacteria."

Then the water should stand in the shade for at least another three hours. After that it can be drunk as 'living water'.

Third ordeal

"So take a drink whenever you feel like it, Papa. In the meantime we shall proceed to the next phase. Usually, for people polluted by the outside world, this whole process takes about nineteen days, Grandfather said, though it is even better to stretch it out over thirty-three days. Since you do not have that kind of time, I have shortened it for you down to three days, but we shall manage. Come with me to another spot — I have set up a particular device there."

We walked about a hundred metres away from the lake, and there amidst a group of trees I saw a place prepared for me to lie down, made of dried grasses. Next to this lay four ropes made of woven nettle fibres or flax.

At one end of each rope there was a noose, while the other was tied to a tree. After I lay down, Volodya put each of my hands and feet through a noose, tugged on them a little and began tightening them with the aid of sticks placed half-way along each rope. After a little tugging, as though trying to literally quarter my body, he jerked each of my hands and feet in turn. I could feel a crunch in my joints. Then he tightened the rope even more, saying:

"Papa, you need to lie like this for an hour on your stomach and an hour on your back. And so that it will not be boring for you and even more beneficial, I shall give you an invigorating massage. And you can just relax, or even go to sleep, if you like."

My son and I went through this procedure two hours each day on all three days.

As I later found out from Grandfather, this procedure served to lubricate all my joints. It is especially important for elderly people. It can even add to one's height, since it straightens out the spinal column. But the main benefit is increased lubrication of the joints. Think about it: when we walk or run or work out in the gymn to pump up our muscles, almost all exercise involves increased pressure on our joints. In Volodya's procedure, though, it is exactly the opposite: the pressure is taken off.

Each time during the stretching procedure, Volodya gave me a massage. On the second day he rubbed down my body with some sort of sweetish juice or tea, and a whole lot of insects crawled over me. I had been told earlier by Anastasia that they served to cleanse the pores of my skin.[1] In our own living conditions, the pores of the skin can be cleansed by going to a Russian *banya* and applying, for example, a birch besom.[2] When a Man steams and sweats, the pores of his skin are cleansed, too.

Interspersed with the stretching procedures we did some fairly common exercises: running, swimming, chinning ourselves on the bough of a tree (using it as one would an exercise bar). About three times a day Volodya suggested I do a handstand, head down, and hold the position for as long as I possibly could. I stood like that, my legs leaning against a tree trunk. This, too, is a rather interesting procedure: a lot of blood rushes to one's face, making it tense up and causing a smoothing of the wrinkles.

For the whole three days we lived on cedar milk, flower pollen, cedar nut oil, berries and a small quantity of dried mushrooms (all this is available in our society). Going through all the procedures thought up by my son and reflecting on how they could be adapted to our conditions, I came to the general conclusion that all this can be done effectively back home. One can even use body-cleansing agents available in pharmacies, as well as making use of diuretic remedies and fasting. It is not difficult to obtain dead water either — all water sold in bottles today is dead water. You can get living water, too, if you have access to a pure wellspring.

You begin to feel the healing effects of these procedures right off.

[1]See Book 1, Chapter 25: "Bugs".

[2]*banya, birch besom* — see footnote 20 in Book 2, Chapter 1: "Alien or man?". Besoms may be made from other types of wood as well — oak or juniper, for example.

A mysterious procedure

But included in this set of procedures was a rather mysterious one, which would be quite a challenge to replicate under our conditions, although maybe someone will have an idea and let me know. I shall describe it in detail. Three times a day — morning, just before lunch and just after three o'clock in the afternoon (more or less) — my son gave me some tea to drink which he had prepared.

Each time when the hour came for me to take the tea, Volodya would run off to his hiding-place and bring back a small jar of this tea, which he invited me to drink, but no more than one swallow at a time. The first time he did this, he said:

"Take a drink of this tea, Papa, and remember how big a swallow you took. As soon as you have drunk it, lie down on the grass, and I shall listen to what is happening with your heart."

I drank the tea and lay down on the grass. Volodya put his little hand on my chest and kept very still. Within a few moments I felt either a warming or a tingling sensation in different parts of my body. My heart began to beat furiously. It wasn't as though it had started beating any faster — I had the sensation of my heart muscles expanding normally, but contracting much more sharply than usual, forcing out the blood.

As I was later informed by specialists, in cases of a vigorous and sharp blood flow through places where the capillary vessels are partially blocked, warming and tingling sensations can be expected.

Volodya listened to my heart-beat for several minutes, and then said:

"Everything is fine, Papa. Your heart can actually withstand an even larger swallow. But it is best not to take any chances. The next time take a slightly smaller swallow."

When I asked my son why he was giving me this tea and what its composition was, he replied as follows:

"This tea, Papa, will give you a great deal of strength, and help you recover from any diseases you may have. But, most importantly, it will enable you to discover the strength and energy you will need for the birth of my sister."

"What, d'you think I don't have enough already?"

"Perhaps. But now you will have strength and energy in abundance, and in the exact balance you need."

"Are they permanent, or will I use them up with the birth of the child?"

"For bearing subsequent children you will need to drink this tea once more. After all, *they* do it this way each time."

"And just who might 'they' be?"

"Sables and other animals. I only studied the sable's actions. It was Grandfather who advised me as to when, at what time and for how many days I needed to watch them in particular."

"And how does Grandfather know about all that?"

"Grandfather, you see, Papa, has all the knowledge of the great wise priests of yore. Even knowledge that has been forgotten by the priests of today. And even knowledge that was secret many thousands of years ago. This tea was taken by the priests before the birth of their children, also before death, so that they could remain immortal."

"What d'you mean, 'before death, so that they could remain immortal'?"

"Well, I mean, so that everyone would think they were dead — whereas, in fact, they only changed bodies and were reincarnated on the spot, and all their information stayed with them. There are other methods of quick reincarnation, but very few that will allow the retention of the information possessed at the time of death. That is why people can be reborn but still have to study life all over again, learn everything right from scratch, and they are unable to compare the present world with the past. And they get confused in their life because they include no knowledge of life and no feelings capable of sensing God."

"But with Grandfather, all the information about the past, you're saying, has been retained?"

"Yes, Papa. Our Grandfather is a great priest and wiseman. There is only one person living on the Earth today who significantly surpasses him in power."

"Where is he living right now, this strongest and wisest one — do you know? You must be talking about the high priest?"

"I am talking about our Mama Anastasia, Papa."

"Anastasia? But how could she have more information and greater knowledge than your great-grandfather?"

"Grandfather says he is hindered by too much information. And he can forget things. But Mama experiences no such hindrance, because there is no information contained in her."

"What d'you mean? Which is it — does she really know more, or has she no knowledge at all?"

"I did not express myself quite accurately, Papa. With Mama Anastasia all the information... how shall I put it?... she has a great deal more, only it is compressed in the form of feelings. And whenever she needs to, she is able to feel in a single moment something that Grandfather might require a day or two, or even more, to think about."

"I can't say I understand everything you've said, but it *is* interesting. Tell me more. What about you? Does this mean that you don't possess information about the past, seeing how you've had to consult with Grandfather?"

"That is correct."

"Why? You mean to say you're mentally inferior to them — Grandfather and Great-grandfather? And what do they tell you about this? Grandfather probably tells you that I'm to blame?"

"Grandfather never told me anything like that."

"But what about Mama? What did she say?"

"I asked Mama why I do not know as much as my fore-bears. And not as much as she, or even you, Papa. And this was her answer:

"'All the truths of the Universe, son, and all the information accumulated right from its pristine origins, has always been available to every Man, nothing hidden. Not everybody is capable of understanding it and making it their own, be-cause their life-goals and the aspirations of their souls do not correspond to those of the Universe. Man has free will in eve-rything, and is free to choose a path other than that of the Universe. But God is free too, as to when, how and to whom He gives a hint. You must not worry about information that is lacking in you. Seek out your dream and know that the whole will be offered to you in full, if the dream that is born within you is worthy of co-creation.'"

"Hmmm... So tell me, Volodya, what do *you* make of all that?"

"Once my dream and life-goal are created in all their detail, all the knowledge I need to turn the dream into reality will be born in me all on its own, without fail."

"But in the meantime, then, you will go on consulting with Grandfather?"

"Yes, with Grandfather, and Mama, and you, and I shall try to ponder life all on my own."

"Does that mean I have to consult with Grandfather about the recipe for the extraordinary tea you've been giving me these past three days?"

"When it comes to the recipe, I can tell you about that my-self."

"Then tell me."

"This recipe was prepared using taiga herbs. So that I would be able to know which herbs to choose, and in what correlation, for three days and nights I observed a sable — one that likewise had an aspiration to be a father. Grandfather told me that the female sable will not allow her mate to approach her if he fails to prepare himself properly. And I observed what herbs he ate during those days, and at what time he chose to pick them. That, too, turned out to be important. All the herbs he ate I gathered as well, only I had to gather a larger store of them, since you, Papa, I can tell, weigh quite a bit more than a sable.

"Once I had gathered samples of a particular kind of herb, I would put them into a vessel and grind them down with a pestle until a juice emerged. All this time I thought only good and pleasant thoughts — about you, Papa, about Mama, and about my future sister. Then I would take the paste which resulted and empty it into a clay jar. I poured water over the jar's contents and added cedar oil so that it formed a film on top. When you drank that swallow of tea, Father, and your heart started beating a bit faster, I could tell the tea had turned out well."

As I listened to my son, I thought: *Not many people have the opportunity to observe a sable in its natural surroundings. But perhaps they could keep watch on what herbs a cat or a dog eats, for example. For that it would be necessary to carry or transport these pets into a forest and follow their behaviour, and, if possible, identify which herbs they ate.*

I was most interested in the tea recipe which my son followed, since just three days' using it produced a palpable effect, while Volodya had indicated a complete therapy course ought to last either nineteen or thirty-three days. That means that after a full-term course, in combination with the other exercises, Man can really free himself from many ills, halt his body's ageing process and rejuvenate himself in some sense of the word. I want to stress that even this three-day application in practice confirms that such an effect is possible. Then there is folk wisdom, too, to take into account, as well as the scientific basis of these procedures.

Of course people have gone to chemists' or drug stores and seen the herbal mixtures our pharmaceutical industry has to offer for the treatment of a variety of ailments.[3] Many know that in Nature there are a whole lot of medicinal plants. But not everyone knows that these can only be really effective, either prophylactically or therapeutically, if they are picked on the right day and at the right time of day.

As to preparing herbal mixtures, along with everything else must be considered the way medicinal herbs correlate with each other. As we can see, there are too many factors that need to be known in order to prepare a mixture like Volodya's. And it is highly doubtful whether any of our herbal healers today knows about all the factors involved.

I very much wanted to take this opportunity of presenting, as a gift to my readers, a recipe for body restoration never before published anywhere in the world, and in a simpler form than Volodya's, so that it will be easily accessible to the majority of people.

Directly my son's three-day therapy course came to an end, he informed me he would like to go to bed earlier than was his custom (it turned out that he barely managed to get two or three hours' sleep a night the past three nights), and he dozed off immediately, while I started heading back toward Anastasia's glade.

I was fascinated by two questions. First, why did our son not possess a knowledge of the past, as did Grandfather? And secondly, was there any way of simplifying the recipe for the tea which he had prepared for me?

---

[3]In Russia today almost all pharmacies carry a large selection of dried medicinal plants, with their healing properties clearly marked on each package.

A vision

Thoughts of food, however, were gradually relegated to the back burner as I began to concentrate more and more on thoughts of my future daughter. On the one hand, it wouldn't be a bad thing at all if Anastasia gave birth to a daughter as well as a son. But on the other hand, when this daughter gets older, she will either have her own Space or inherit the Space created by my son and face the same problems Volodya is having to deal with right now. Besides, who could she possibly marry, here in the taiga?

She could go off into our world, but that wouldn't be easy either. It would mean leaving her own Space and her loyal animal friends. And I can't imagine any young man agreeing to come and live with her in the taiga. It's not all that comfortable here in the wilds for someone from the outside. And, to be honest about it, that includes me. It is interesting to talk with Anastasia — I would even say her company is alluring. When I'm with her, I feel a sense of peace and joy in my heart. But when I'm left all alone and she's not around, I feel uncomfortable, to say the least — even a bit fearful.

The creatures treat Anastasia and our son quite differently from me. Of course they don't attack me, but whenever we meet, they still regard me with an air of suspicion. I once attempted — in Anastasia's presence — to command the squirrels to bring me some cedar cones. I made the same gestures as Anastasia, but there was no reaction from the squirrels. Another time I tried calling the she-wolf. Just like Anastasia, I held out my hand to her, then clapped it against my thigh. But instead of running toward me, she stood rooted to the spot, and her hackles stood on end in a show of aggression. And I lost any desire to further communicate with these creatures. I realised that they could be loyal only to one specific Man in perpetuity.

So it could turn out that some young man comes to see our daughter in the taiga and he will not feel comfortable in her Space. Volodya has not given sufficient thought to his sister's future. Turns out he feels sorry for the creatures, but apparently not for his sister. And I didn't think about it either — I absent-mindedly gave him encouragement.

Immersed in these thoughts, I was surprised to discover that I had already arrived at Anastasia's glade. No sooner had I taken a few steps in the direction of the familiar dugout than I noticed Anastasia herself standing there, her body half-turned to me, combing her long hair with her hands. I stopped dead in my tracks: she did not look at all like the same woman I had known for the past ten years. And when she turned to face me, my legs became jelly, my heart began throbbing and I realised I could not move from the spot.

Just ten to fifteen paces from me stood a woman who looked the picture of a fairy-tale vision. She was wearing a long, sheer, light-coloured dress down to her ankles, almost like a ball gown, gathered with a belt around her slender waist. Her head was crowned with a wreath woven of grasses and flowers, like a diadem. Her golden hair hung in wavelets around her shoulders. But that wasn't all! Her stately figure and face were so beautiful as to defy any possible description.

I stood there, afraid to move, my gaze unblinkingly fixed on Anastasia. It seemed as though if I took my eyes away I would lose consciousness. My head began spinning, but I continued to gaze at her without blinking. I found myself digging my nails forcefully into my hand, seeking escape in pain from this extraordinary state of mind. But I hardly felt any pain at all.

And as this uniquely beautiful woman gradually and graciously approached me, I lost all sensation, not just of pain but of any part of my physique. She slowly came right up to me, and I recall feeling the enchanting fragrance of her body. I could sense her light breathing and... I lost consciousness.

When I woke up I was lying on the ground. Anastasia was sitting beside me, massaging my temples and the bridge of my nose. Her diadem-wreath was gone, and her hair was brushed back and tied with a blade of grass. I felt an almost complete calm as I gazed into those tender greyish-blue eyes which had become so dear to me. And I finally came to myself upon hearing her voice:

"What happened to you, Vladimir? Did you get overtired, or did our son somehow upset you?"

"Our son... No, quite to the contrary, he has been giving me treatments these past three days. We went through a series of exercises."

"And you overexerted yourselves?"

"Volodya did. He fell asleep. By contrast, I've begun to feel very good indeed."

"Then why did you lose consciousness? Your heart was throbbing and has still not completely calmed down."

"Because... Oh, Anastasia, why did you dress up that way? Your hair's somehow different. And the way you walked as you approached me — that was unusual, too."

"I wanted to do something nice for you, Vladimir. After all, you are more accustomed to look at women in fancy clothes. I thought you and I could take a walk together through the taiga or along the lakeshore. And here you are lying down. If you want to have a rest, let us go to the dug-out, and there you can have a nap."

"First let's go and take a walk, as you proposed," I said as I rose to my feet. "Only you, Anastasia, walk behind me, please."

"Why?"

"Because... Yes, I am more accustomed to looking at women in fancy clothes, as you say. But it is better for me if you don't dress up that way, or wear your hair like that, or adorn yourself like that."

"You did not like the way I looked, Vladimir?" enquired Anastasia, as she trotted along behind me.

"That's not it. I liked it very much. Only, in future, do it just one step at a time. Your hair first, for example. And then spend some time wearing it that way. Then you can put on your diadem-wreath, and a day or two later the dress. Only without the belt to start with, and afterward you can put on the belt. You see, if you do everything at once, it's really hard for me to get accustomed to. It looks strange."

"Strange? Does that mean you did not recognise me, Vladimir?"

"I recognised you. But... It's just that I was simply overwhelmed with your beauty, Anastasia."

"Aha, you admit it! You admit it! That means you really think I am beautiful? Eh?"

I felt her hands resting on my shoulders, and I stopped. Then I closed my eyes, turned around and replied:

"You, Anastasia, are not just beautiful. You are..."

She pressed herself against me, putting her head on my shoulder.

"Our son, Anastasia," I went on, in a whisper, "would like to have a little sister."

"And I would like you and me, Vladimir, to have a daughter," Anastasia quietly responded.

"May she have your looks, Anastasia!"

"And may our daughter be like you..."

I shall not describe that night. Or the following morning. They are beyond description. But I shall say one thing to my men-readers: if any of you manage to see a goddess in the woman you know, your days and nights — many, many days and nights, in fact — will be divine. All the miseries of the past will vanish before them. And there will be no more storms to darken your day. I'm not talking about sentimentality here, nor about beautiful words and professions of love. The whole point is...

In any case, let each figure it out for themselves, if they can and wish to do so.

CHAPTER FIVE

Divine nutrition

It was only several days later that I remembered I wanted to find out from Anastasia the recipe for the therapeutic tea, as well as the overall method of correct nutrition or dietetics for my readers. It's a good thing I remembered. It seems that Anastasia knew about an unusual — I might say, unique — method of nutrition which can be applied even to city living conditions.

To my surprise, instead of giving me the tea recipe right off, Anastasia began talking about Man's capabilities, about patients and healers. We had spoken of this on several other occasions, but what she had to tell me this time was indeed interesting.

"Reality, Vladimir, must be defined only through one's self. Every Man living on the Earth today is capable of seeing into the lives of people thousands of years ago, of looking into the future, and of creating his own future. All have this tremendous ability within themselves. It just needs to be understood. Once it is understood, then nobody can lead them away from the truth. People will come into harmony with each other, and endless warfare will cease.

"A lot of efforts have been made to distort past reality. The possibility of distortion arises when Man abandons his own reasoning powers and forms constructs of the past based on somebody else's words and conclusions."

"It is not entirely clear to me, Anastasia, how every Man on the Earth can arrive at a knowledge of people living in centuries past, let alone past millennia. There is a whole science, too, exclusively devoted to studying the history of mankind. But even today scholars argue over Man's origin and purpose. Historical events are interpreted in different ways."

"'In different ways' — does that mean there are correct and incorrect interpretations? Or perhaps there is some distortion in the way they *all* describe the past? As a rule, the distortions are introduced for someone's particular benefit. But when you, all by yourself, recreate scenes of the past within yourself, you will see the truth — you will determine your purpose and place in the Universe."

"But how, for example, would I be able to see historical scenes of thousands of years ago all on my own?"

"You can picture them through logical thinking. And even the life of the Vedruss civilisation will appear to you."

"And what should I think logically about?"

"About images of people you have seen over the half-century of your life, and the changes that have taken place in them."

"It's still not too clear to me just how I should be thinking."

"It will become clear if you are not too lazy to think. Come, Vladimir, let us begin together, and you can continue on your own, and every Man may recreate scenes of the past, in order to integrate the very best parts into his future."

"All right then, but you be the first to start."

"I shall begin. Look hard and, if you can, add details — they are important. Today you see a whole lot of hospitals and pharmacies with medicines for thousands of ailments."

"Yes, that's something everyone can see. What of it?"

"Do you recall that just thirty years ago there were fewer of them?"

"Yes, of course."

"And how many were there a hundred or two hundred years ago?"

"A lot fewer. Everybody knows that modern medical science is only a little over two hundred years old."

"You see, your own logic has led you to a conclusion: not too long ago there were no hospitals at all. Now think, and recall: who treated people in cases of illness?"

"Who?"

"You yourself lived in a village and saw how your grandmother gave your father and mother herb teas to drink."

"In that village it wasn't just my grandmother who could bring about cures — there were others too."

"And in every human settlement there were most certainly people who gathered and preserved therapeutic herbs. And every Man could obtain help right away, whether he came down with a minor ailment or even a serious disease. And payment for help was a pittance, often just a simple 'thank you' sufficed."

"Well, sure, they were neighbours, after all. And there were plenty of herbs to be found all around."

"Yes, there were very many useful herbs. And many people were aware of the properties of these herbs."

"Of course they were. I myself knew about some of them, but now I've forgotten."

"You see, you have forgotten. Many people have forgotten. What does a Man do today if he gets a scratch or a cut?"

"He goes to a pharmacy, buys a bandage or a band-aid and sticks it on the wound."

"He spends time getting to the pharmacy and spends money when he is there. By contrast, in the past, every child knew that if you apply a plantain leaf directly to a wound, the wound will quickly heal and there will be no infection."

"I know that too, but today in many places the herbs are contaminated. All around, you find noxious fumes from cars, dust, acid rain..."

"Yes, you are right. But that is not the point. When we talk about images of the past, you could draw the conclusion

that Man's knowledge of curing people in the past was superior to that of people today."

"It would seem that way."

"I hear a note of doubt or uncertainty in your voice,
Vladimir. In that case the image will not appear before you.
You must be absolutely certain in the force of your confidence. Or in your rejection. Continue to pursue the course
of logic."

"You see, Anastasia, all logic, too, tells me that Man's knowledge in the area of folk medicine in the past was significantly
greater than that possessed by people today. One might even
say, immeasurably greater. It follows that the services effected on the basis of this knowledge were significantly more perfected than today. But somehow it is challenging to suddenly
find that all our modern hospitals, pharmacies and medical
institutions are completely superfluous. It simply boggles the
mind!

"When someone in the Vedruss civilisation — our ances-
tor — came down with an ailment, he would eat a herb or
drink a tea, and the ailment was gone. When someone in *our*
civilisation takes ill, he goes to the hospital, pays a fee to be
seen by a doctor, the doctor prescribes some kind of pills or
shots, and the patient has to pay again for the drugs, often
quite dearly so. And then in lots of cases the drugs turn out
to be counterfeit. Officials from the Ministry of Health say
that up to 30% of the drugs sold at our pharmacies are counterfeit.

"And then a whole bunch of terrible new diseases keep popping up. It's as though someone deliberately erased the perfect knowledge we once had and replaced it with something
less efficient or even illusory. Moreover, official medicine still
today treats folk healers with a fair degree of scepticism, probably because it sees them as competition. But why do not the
state and society realise that for hundreds and thousands of

years mankind has efficiently healed itself through folk medicine, accumulating a huge amount of experience over this time, and hence this deserves to be developed and studied? And, in the final analysis, to be taught in the schools?

"But that would mean all the businesses involved in modern medicine would collapse... incredible! Simply incredible, Anastasia! I think I'm beginning to understand: modern medicine is not as much about curing people as about running a business! And if it's business we're talking about, that means that all the companies making pills find it much more profitable when people are ill. The more sick people there are, the more income will kick in for the drug companies. By the laws of business, in such a situation the number of sick people will quickly begin to steadily increase. It's a vicious circle. I'm becoming more and more convinced that health care in the distant past was much more rational and effective than today. Only there are a few historical facts that are standing in the way of a final conclusion."

"What kind of facts, Vladimir?"

"Well, for instance, history has recorded epidemic outbreaks of plagues, smallpox and leprosy. Some history textbooks say that whole settlements died out. Did that really happen?"

"Yes, it did."

"But now, through he help of modern medicine, the plagues have been beaten, along with cholera and smallpox. For example, they inoculate everyone against smallpox and that's the end of it. That means that the folk healers of the past were defeated by these diseases, while modern medicine has succeeded."

"That is not true, Vladimir. Take a closer look at the timeframes and put simple facts together. These epidemic outbreaks you speak of began happening at a time when folk healers were subjected to persecution. Many of them were

even put to death. During the occult ages[1] they were seen as a
threat to the authorities. Both then and now it was believed
that pagans worshipped Nature and were unspiritual people.
This is not true: pagans respected Nature as the creation of
God. And they had knowledge of many of the Divine creations which people are ignorant of today."

"That's enough, Anastasia. I no longer have any doubts. It
is plain that modern medical science is a long ways from the
science of folk medicine. I'm convinced of that. But why did
you go to such pains to persuade me?"

"It was not just for you. I wanted your readers, too, to be
able to understand by comparing facts."

"But what for?"

"When one fact is proved beyond a shadow of a doubt, other indisputable conclusions will come about. They may seem
incredible, but please do not be so easily amazed, Vladimir."

"What incredible conclusions, for example?"

"First, answer this question. Tell me how people — the
majority of people — explain how mankind in ancient times
possessed such colossal information about Nature."

"What d'you mean, how? If you're talking about the prescriptions of folk medicine, it's quite clear they were passed
down from generation to generation."

"All right, that may be. But I think you will agree that for
each of the thousands of prescriptions, there had to be an
original author."

"According to logic, of course, there had to be, but now it is
no longer possible to trace the authorship of these prescriptions."

"It is possible! All the knowledge of the grand creation
was imparted by the Creator to each and every one without

[1]For more information on the occult ages, see Book 6, Chapter 8:
"Occultism".

exception. This I shall prove to you, Vladimir, and to every-body. Do not be too hasty to dismiss what I say as incred-ible."

"I shall try not to. Go on."

"People think that originally Man was many times more feeble-minded than today. But that is not true, Vladimir. People of pristine origins had Divine knowledge right from the beginning."

"But what d'you mean, 'from the beginning', Anastasia? What, did God Himself write out prescriptions for a whole bunch of herbal treatments? Historians' descriptions allude to mankind gradually accumulating its knowledge over the centuries."

"But to pursue the course of logic to its end, that particular allusion would lead to a different conclusion."

"What kind of conclusion?"

"It would follow from that that Man is not the perfect crea-tion of God but the most underdeveloped of all creatures that ever lived on the Earth!"

"How does that follow?"

"Think about it. Your dog knows what herbs she needs to eat when she comes down with an ailment. And a cat will know to run to the forest to find a herb she requires. But nobody wrote them a prescription. A bee knows all about ex-tracting nectar from a flower, building a honeycomb and stor-ing honey in it, and gathering pollen. And what raising the next generation is all about. If one link in the chain of knowl-edge the bee family is endowed with should be removed, the whole family would die out.

"But bees continue to exist today. And that can only mean one thing: the Creator has given them all the knowledge they need right from the start, right at the moment of their crea-tion. And that is why the bees have not died out, but have lived for millions of years, and are still building their unique honeycombs even today, just as in the first moment of their creation. And the ants, too, continue to build their homes. And flowers continue to unfold their petals with the advance of each new dawn, just as on the first day of their creation. And the apple, pear and cherry trees know exactly what kind of juices they need from the ground to grow their fruit. All information is given to them right at their inception, right at the moment of their creation. And Man is no exception."

"Yes... Incredible. All logic really does lead to that conclusion. And that means... Hold on — just where is all this knowledge right now?"

"It is preserved in every single Man. And the therapeutic recipe for the healing herbal tea is one that every Man is free to compile for himself."

"But how?"

"You see, Vladimir, God gave it to Man right from the beginning. It is capable of curing a great many diseases of the flesh and prolonging life. It is extremely simple, and at the same time not so simple. Man should be able to figure it out with his mind. Let me start with some pre-history."

In the Vedruss civilisation everybody lived to be more than a hundred years old. And they knew no diseases of the flesh. They nourished themselves according to God's prescription. Not arbitrarily and not haphazardly but with the greatest thoughtfulness the Creator specially arranged it so that the herbs, vegetables, berries and fruits did not ripen all at once, but one after the other in a strict sequence.

One ripened in the early spring, others over the summer, or later in the autumn. Their ripening time was determined by the moment when the specific fruit, vegetable or herb could offer the greatest benefit to Man. A Man living on his own domain, feeding himself as God prescribed, could not take ill. The type of food and the time of taking it had been determined for Man by God. Man himself decided the quantity of food, but not through reason — he ate as much as he liked. And his body could accurately determine, down to the gram, the required quantity of food.

In the autumn each family put up stores for the winter: berries, root vegetables, herbs, nuts and mushrooms. Over the winter, in every household a plate stood on the table, with little piles of produce from the summer harvest. All the members of the family were involved in their own activities, but whenever they felt hungry or thirsty, they would go over to the table and take what they needed without thinking about it. Note, Vladimir: they took what they needed *without thinking.* Their bodies knew exactly what kind of food was needed and in what quantity — everyone had been endowed with this ability by God. This ability can be revived now. All that is needed is information.

I have adapted the Vedruss method of nutrition for people of today. Try it yourself, and encourage others to try it. It goes as follows.

A Man living in a modern apartment needs to acquire a small quantity — a hundred or two hundred grams each — of all the vegetables, fruits and edible herbs growing in the region where he lives.

Before using any of this produce he should go a whole day without eating, drinking only spring water, and having a glass of red beet juice for lunch. After drinking the beet juice it is better not to leave his home. The stomach and bowels will start undergoing an intensive cleansing process.

Upon awakening the following morning and feeling hungry, he should be able to take any vegetable, herb or piece of fruit and put it on a small plate. After sitting down at the table, he should carefully observe what is lying on the plate, sniff it, lick it and then eat it with an unhurried chewing. It is best to be alone in the room during this time, isolated from the sounds of the artificial world.

The feeling of hunger may not disappear after eating a single piece of food, or it may reappear after a short period of time. In that case he should select a second piece and eat it in the same manner as the first.

Man should take all the produce he has obtained and sample them in any sequence at short intervals.

The time for sampling any particular food is determined by the sensation of hunger.

The taking of food should definitely begin in the morning.

By the end of this day a Man should have sampled all locally grown produce. If there is a large variety available and one day is insufficient, the sampling can extend to the following day.

This procedure is extremely important. It will give many people's bodies, perhaps for the first time in their lives, a chance to become acquainted with the taste qualities and properties of the local produce, and to determine how needful it is to Man at a given moment and in what quantity.

Once the body has become familiar with all the produce, one should cut each vegetable into small pieces and lay them out on a large plate. Small clumps of greens and berries should also be put out, either alongside or on another plate. Any produce that will quickly spoil on the plate should be immersed in spring water.

Also on the table one should put honey, flower pollen, cedar oil and spring water. Man may go about his own daily affairs, but when he feels hungry he can go over to the table and pick up an item he likes (either with his hands or with a wooden spoon) and eat it.

It is possible some of the food may be eaten up completely, while the rest may be left untouched. This means that your personal wise physician and nutritionist — your body which was given to you by the Creator — selected for you what you needed at that moment, while what you did not need was left untouched.

The uneaten produce need not be put again on the table the following day. But after three days a complete variety should once again be displayed. It is possible that one's body will need something different by then.

In time Man will be able to determine which items can be temporarily excluded from his diet, so as not to waste his efforts in obtaining them. But it is possible that after a period of time his body will indeed have need of them again, and so from time to time one should lay out on the table as wide a variety as possible.

I know that people living in your world often need to be away from their dwellings, but even here one can adapt. For example, one can make or acquire a small birch-bark container, in which to put a portion of the food from the table. One's body will choose what is most required.

In case of an extended trip, one's body needs to become familiar with the produce available in the new territory, since, in spite of identical names, there may be significant taste differences.

In this method of nutrition, Vladimir, it is important to grasp one essential point: it is not only the animals that are able to determine which kinds of food will be most beneficial to their bodies at a given moment and in what quantity. This knowledge is present, too, within every single Man.

Our son thought up everything correctly: to prepare the healing tea for you from taiga herbs, he decided to observe a sable. But if you yourself knew the taste of every herb, your body would be able to determine and select the herbs you need far more accurately than the sable.

When you get back to your apartment, allow your body to get to know the taste of all easily available produce. Do not mix the food together or add salt, otherwise your body will not be able to determine the value and significance of the produce.

This method by which any Man can compile his own dietary régime or recipe for healthful nutrition seemed to me to be most original and logical. The body's needs — in terms of quantity and variety of produce — will naturally differ from one individual to the next. Consequently, there cannot be a single recipe or dietary régime which is the same for all. But through the aid of the method proposed by Anastasia, every Man can make up his own individual régime, which will be as accurate and useful as possible for him.

It appears as though man-made recipes and prescriptions are not always beneficial to one's health. Instead, they tend to be technology-based and more convenient for the manufacturers and organisers of our modern nutrition industry. Take McDonald's, for example — one of the most powerful and influential corporations, known around the globe —

inculcating in the whole world a taste for uniform hamburgers and cheeseburgers along with packages of fried potatoes, roping in everybody under a single unitary norm. Such a system undoubtedly works very well to the manufacturer's advantage — uniform products, uniform equipment and preparation technology. How far removed such uniformity is from the natural method of nutrition, and how harmful!

More and more people all over the planet are becoming aware of this. Wednesday, 16 October 2002 (the UN's World Food Day),[2] became the annual official day of protest against McDonald's — a protest against the promotion of junk products under the guise of food, the use of aggressive child-oriented advertising campaigns, the cruel exploitation of workers, unethical treatment of animals, destruction of the environment and the world dominance of large corporations over our lives.

More and more, McDonald's is being held up by a worldwide circle of protesters as a symbol of contemporary capitalism. One after another, all across the globe lawsuits are being brought against American corporations dealing in 'junk food' — McDonald's, Kentucky Fried Chicken, Burger King and Wendy's — on behalf of millions of consumers led astray by the systematic and unethical promotion of harmful food products. These people have consequently suffered from obesity, heart ailments and a variety of other serious health

[2] *World Food Day* (also known as *World Nutrition Day*) — established in 1979 by the member countries of the United Nations Food and Agricultural Organisation (FAO) to raise awareness of world poverty and hunger and to commemorate the founding of the FAO on 16 October 1945 in the city of Québec (Canada). A specific theme is selected for each year's celebration. The Worldwide Anti-McDonald's protest is an independent movement which chose their annual protest day to coincide with World Food Day. According to their literature, the Worldwide Anti-McDonald's Day has been marked since 1985.

problems. Concern over this health threat is growing everywhere in Europe and the USA, exacerbated by mad cow disease and the use of genetically modified feed, as well as direct
consumption of genetically modified produce (e.g., potatoes
and corn) and their traces in other products (chocolate, pas-
try etc.).

But is it only our nutritional system that is constructed with
somebody's particular profit motive in mind? What about
our contemporary governmental institutions?

Take, for example, our modern democratic society — how
ideally suited is it to human life? I was most interested to
hear what Anastasia would have to say about this.

"Tell me, Anastasia, if someone could construct a nutritional system for their own advantage at the expense of millions of people, I wonder whether our social order might have
been deliberately set up with a similar motive."

"Indeed it has. Think about it, Vladimir: ages pass, and
the names of your societal structures change, but their *raison
d'être* remains the same — the exploitation of people."

"Well, it hasn't always been the same. For example, we
used to have slavery, and now we have democracy. I think,
under democracy there is far less exploitation than when we
had slavery."

"Vladimir, would you like me to show you a scene from the
past and tell you a parable?"

"I would."

"Then look and see."

CHAPTER SIX

Demon Cratius

The slaves walked slowly in single file, every one of them carrying a polished stone. Four lines of them, each line stretching a kilometre and a half long, from the stone quarries to the site where construction on the walled city had begun, under the watchful eyes of armed guards — one military guard for every ten slaves.[1]

Off to one side, on the pinnacle of a thirteen-metre-high 'mountain' crafted out of polished stones, sat Cratius, one of the high priests. For the past four months he had been silently observing the construction activity. Nobody distracted him, not a single person dared interrupt his contemplation, even with a sideways glance.

Both slaves and guards accepted this artificial mountain with its throne on top as a fixed feature of the landscape. And nobody paid attention to the figure either sitting motionless on the throne or walking to and fro around the lookout platform atop the 'mountain'. Cratius had set himself the task of restructuring the state, consolidating the power of the priests for a millennium, subjugating to them all the people of the Earth, turning all without exception (including national rulers) into slaves of the priests.

---

[1] Anastasia's narrative is told in the first part of this chapter without quotation-marks.

One day Cratius came down from his throne, leaving a double in his place. The priest changed his clothes and took off his wig. He gave orders to the captain of the guard to have him bound in chains like a simple slave and placed in the line behind a strong young slave named Nard.

Looking into the faces of the various slaves, Cratius had noticed that this young man in particular had a penetrating and purposeful look, not a wandering or detached gaze as did many of the others. Nard's countenance alternated between excitement and intense contemplation. *That means he's hatching some kind of plan,* the priest realised, but he wanted confirmation of the accuracy of this observation.

For two days running Cratius followed Nard's every move, silently hauling the stones, sitting beside him at mealtimes and sleeping next to him in the barracks. On the third night, directly the *Sleep!* command had been given, Cratius turned to the young slave and in a tone of bitterness and despair whispered to no one in particular:

"Will this situation keep up the rest of our lives?"

The priest watched as the young slave gave a shudder, and suddenly turned to face him. His eyes were sparkling, which was noticeable even in the dim torchlight of the cavernous barracks.

"It won't last much longer," the young slave whispered back. "I've been working out a plan. And you, old fellow, can be part of it!"

"What sort of plan?" the priest asked with a sigh of indifference.

Nard began to explain with an air of confidence and enthusiasm:

"You see, old man, soon you and I and all of us will be free men instead of slaves. Figure it out for yourself: there's just one guard for every ten of us. And one guard, too, for every fifteen women slaves who do the cooking and sewing. When the time comes, if we all fall upon the guards at once, we can overpower them. It makes no difference that the guards are armed and we're in chains. We outnumber them ten to one, and our chains can also be used as weapons, to shield us from the blows of their swords. We'll disarm all the guards, tie them up and seize their weapons."

"Hold on there, young man," Cratius sighed again, and added with feigned indifference: "Your plan isn't completely thought through. Sure you can disarm the guards watching over us, but it won't be long before the ruler sends in replacements — a whole army, maybe — and he'll have the insurgents killed."

"I've thought of that, too, old man. We'll have to choose a time when the army's not around. And that time is coming. We've all noticed how the army's preparing for a campaign. They're getting provisions ready for a three-month trek. That means that in three months the army will arrive at its destination and engage the enemy in combat. It will be weakened in battle, but it will be victorious, and bring back many new slaves. They're already building new barracks to house them. We have to start disarming the guards just as soon as our ruler's army goes into battle. The couriers will need at least a month to go call it home, and it will take at least three months after that for the weakened army to return. By the time the four months are up we'll be ready to meet them. We'll have at least as many fighters as there are in the army. The slaves they seize will want to join us when they see what's happened. I've thought it all out in advance, old man."

"I see, young fellow, with your plan you can disarm the guards and overpower the army," the priest answered, already sounding more cheerful, and then added: "But what will become of the slaves after that, and what will happen with the rulers, the guards and the soldiers?"

"I haven't given too much thought to that. Only one thing comes to mind, though: whoever was a slave in the past will become a free man. Whoever's not a slave today will be a slave tomorrow," replied Nard with some hesitation, as though thinking aloud.

"But what about the priests? Tell me, young man, after your victory, will they be slaves or not?"

"The priests? Haven't thought about that either. But now I'm thinking: the priests can stay where they are. The slaves and rulers listen to them. Sometimes they're hard to understand, but I get the feeling they're harmless. Let them keep on telling their stories about the gods, but we know best how to live our lives and have a good time."

"Have a good time — that's great," responded the priest, and pretended he couldn't wait to get to sleep.

But there was no sleep for Cratius that night. Only contemplation. *Sure,* he thought, *the simplest course of action would be to report this to the ruler, and have them seize this young slave — he's clearly the chief instigator. But that won't solve the problem. The slaves will always have the desire to be freed from bondage. New leaders will emerge, new plans will be hatched, and as long as that goes on, the main threat to the state will always be from within.*

Cratius was faced with the challenge of working out a plan to enslave the whole world. He realised there was no way he could attain his goal through physical compulsion alone. What he needed to do was exert a psychological influence on every single individual, on whole nations of people. He had to bring about the thought of every single human being to the notion that *slavery is the highest bliss.* He had to launch a self-developing programme to disorient whole nations in space, time and ideas — especially in their literal perception of reality.

Cratius' thought was working faster and faster, he was no longer conscious of his body, or the heavy chains on his arms and legs. And all of a sudden, like a bolt of lightning, a programme came to his thought. Even though all the details were still to be worked out, and he could not yet explain it to anyone else, he could already feel it within, exploding off the scale. Cratius was now feeling himself to be the omnipotent ruler of the world.

Lying on his bunk in chains, he was full of self-exultation: *Tomorrow morning, when they're escorting us all to work, I'll give the secret signal and have the guards captain take me out of the line and remove the chains. I'll finalise my programme, say a few words and the world will start to change. Incredible! Just a few words, and the whole world will be subject to me, to my thoughts. God really has given to Man a power unequalled in the Universe — the power of human thought. It brings forth words which can change the course of history.*

The situation's turned out very well indeed. The slaves have prepared their plan of insurrection. It's logical, this plan, and is clearly capable of leading to an interim result very favourable to them. But with just a few words I shall ensure that not only they, but their future descendants, and the rulers of the Earth too, will be slaves for millennia to come.

In the morning, on Cratius' signal, the captain of the guard freed him from his chains. And the very next day the five other priests, along with the pharaoh, were invited to his observation platform. Cratius began his speech before the gathering as follows:

"What you are about to hear must not be noted down or passed along by any of you. There are no walls around us, and my words will be heard by no one but you. I have thought up a way of turning all people living on the Earth into slaves of our pharaoh. That is not something one can do even with the aid of vast numbers of troops and exhausting wars. But I shall accomplish it with a few simple sentences. All I need do is utter them and just two days later you will see how the world has begun to change.

"Take a look down there and you will see long lines of slaves in chains, each slave carrying a stone. They are guarded by a host of soldiers. The more slaves there are, the better for the state — or so we always thought. But the more slaves there are, the more we have to be afraid of their rebelling. So we increase the size of our guard.

"We are obliged to feed our slaves well, otherwise they will not be able to perform their heavy manual labour. But still they are lazy and inclined to rebellion. See how slowly they move, and the guards have become lazy and do not bother using their whips to beat even the strongest and healthiest slaves. But they will soon be moving much more quickly. They won't need any guards. The guards themselves will be turned into slaves. This can be effected in the following way:

"Before sunset today heralds will be sent out everywhere to proclaim the pharaoh's decree: *With the dawn of the new day all slaves will be granted complete freedom. For each stone brought to the city, the free men will receive one coin. The coins may be exchanged for food, clothing, housing, a palace in town, or even a whole town. From here on in, you are free people.*"

After the priests had let Cratius' words sink in, one of them, the eldest, said:

"You are a demon, Cratius! The demonry resulting from your plan will cover most of the nations of the world."

"So, I may indeed be a demon, and what I have thought up, people in the future may call democracy."

At sunset the decree was proclaimed to the slaves. They were astounded. Many of them could not sleep at night, thinking about the new and happy life that lay ahead of them.

The next morning the priests and the pharaoh once again climbed up to the lookout platform atop the artificial mountain. They could not believe the scene unfolding before their eyes. Thousands of former slaves chasing one after the other, hauling the same stones as before. Dripping with sweat, many of them were carrying two stones apiece. Others with only one stone in their hands, were literally running, kicking up the dust as they ran. Some of the guards were also hauling stones. These people, who now considered themselves free — after all, they were no longer in chains — strove to obtain as many of the sought-after coins as they could, so that they could build a happy life for themselves.

Cratius remained at his post on the platform for several months after that, continuing to observe with satisfaction what was going on below. The transformation was colossal. Some of the slaves had organised themselves into groups and built themselves carts. Then they piled stones on top of the carts, and pushed them along, their skin covered in sweat.

They will invent many more devices, Cratius thought to himself with satisfaction. *Internal services have already started — food and water delivery. Some slaves have been eating right on the go, not wanting to waste time going back to the barracks for a meal, and paying for the food delivery with the coins they've earned. Wow! They've also got doctors going around, offering help to people with physical needs right on the spot — also for coins. And they've appointed themselves traffic regulators. Soon they'll be choosing their own rulers and judges. Let them choose: after all, they consider themselves free now, whereas nothing has really changed — they're still hauling the same stones as before...*

And so they have been running, down through the millennia right up to the present day, through the dust, sweating to carry the heavy stones. And today the descendants of those slaves still keep up their senseless running.

"You're probably thinking of ordinary working people, Anastasia?" I observed. "Sure, anybody could agree with that. But you can't apply the term *slaves* to heads of corporations, or government officials, or entrepreneurs."

"Do you see a difference, Vladimir? If so, tell me what it is."

"On the one hand you've got people labouring and hauling stones like slaves. The others are *in charge* of the hauling — or, in today's terms, managing the operation."

"But managing, after all, is still work, and often more complex work than slaves hauling stones."

"Well, in a sense you're right: entrepreneurs have a bit more thinking to do. Their thought is occupied with their work from morning 'til night. So, does that mean that the pharaohs, the presidents and chancellors are slaves, too?"

"Yes, that is correct. Even the priests have become slaves, the ones who dreamt up this whole fateful scheme."

"But if there are slaves, there must also be slave-owners. Who are they, if you aren't including even the priests in this category?"

"The slave-owner is the artificial world people have been creating themselves. And the guards sit within most people's minds or bodies, whipping them and making them earn coins."

"It's a sad scene indeed," I observed, "and it looks as though there's no way out. Over the past thousands of years empires have come and gone, religions and laws have changed, but in fact nothing has really changed: just as Man was a slave before, he remains one now. Tell me, is there any way this situation can be corrected?"

"There is."

"How? And who can do it?"

"The image."

"What d'you mean, *image*? What kind of image?"

"The image that offers people a different situation. Judge for yourself, Vladimir: people who control the world today through money believe that only power and money can bring happiness to Man. And all the people out there striving to earn a few coins have convinced them that they are right. But often — very often, in fact — the winners in this senseless rat-race are the ones who suffer the most. They reach illusory heights and feel, more acutely than others, the whole senselessness of their life. I shall show you a scene from the future — go ahead and describe it. Let it be played out in real life."

CHAPTER SEVEN

The billionaire

The billionaire John Heitzman was dying on the forty-second storey of his office tower. The whole floor had been converted into his personal apartment. Two bedrooms, a work-out gymn, a swimming pool, a dining room and two studies had comprised his refuge for the past three years. During this time he had not left his apartment even once. Not once had he taken the express lift down to where the core of his financial and industrial empire was in full operation. Not once had he gone up to the roof, where his personal helicopter was on standby, replete with a full crew awaiting his command.

Three times a week John Heitzman retreated to one of his studies to receive four of his closest associates. At these brief sessions, which lasted no more than forty minutes, he listened to their reports with some indifference, and occasionally issued brief instructions. The billionaire's orders were never a subject for discussion — they were simply carried out swiftly and to the letter. The book value of the empire under his exclusive control kept increasing by an average 16.5% annually. Even over the past six months, when Heitzman ceased convening even his tri-weekly sessions altogether, the ledgers showed no decline in profits. The system he had created continued to run smoothly with no glitches.

Nobody knew the billionaire's true financial worth. His name was hardly ever mentioned in the press. Heitzman held strictly to the rule: *Money hates trouble.*

As a young man he had been admonished by his father along these lines:

"Let those upstart politicians strut their stuff on the TV screens and in the pages of the press. Let the presidents and governors spout their addresses to the people, assuring them all's well. Let the billionaires in the public eye go gallivanting about the country with their fancy cars and bodyguards. That is not a course, my dear John, you yourself should follow. You should always remain in the shadows and use your power, the power of money, to control governments and presidents, the wealthy and the poor, in a variety of different countries. But they must never guess who is controlling them.

"The plan is simple in the extreme. I was the one who created the Monetary Fund, which lists the names of many different investors. In actual fact seventy percent of the fund's capital has been invested by me under different names. On the surface, as far as the dimwit masses are concerned, the fund was created for the support of developing countries. In actual fact I created it as a device for collecting 'tribute-money' from all the countries involved.

"Here's an example. Let's say an armed conflict breaks out between two sides. One of them (more often, both) needs money. Let them have it — it will be repaid with interest. Or some country is experiencing a social upheaval and, again, money is required. Let them have it — it will be repaid with interest. Or two political forces come into conflict; one of them will get money through our agents, and once again it will be repaid with interest. Russia alone pays us an annual sum of three billion dollars."

At age twenty, John Heitzman had especially enjoyed these discussions with his father. Despite his earlier severity and reticence to talk, one day the father summoned John to his office and invited him to make himself comfortable in a soft armchair by the fireplace, while he himself poured a cup of his son's favourite coffee with cream and asked with a spark of genuine interest:

"How are your college studies going, John?"

"They're not always that interesting, Dad. I get the feeling the professors aren't too good at giving a clear and comprehensible explanation of the laws of economics."

"Good. An apt assessment. But more precisely: professors today can't explain the laws of economics because they haven't the faintest idea of them themselves. They think economics is the domain of economists. But it isn't. World economics is under the control of psychologists, philosophers and high-stakes players.

"When I was twenty, my father — your granddad, John — let me into the secrets of the management process. Now that *you're* twenty, I think you're worthy of inheriting this knowledge."

"Thanks, Dad," replied John. Thus began, in these fireside chats, lessons in the laws of economics one never hears about at university. The father taught his son using his own unique method. The whole educational process was conducted in these heart-to-heart conversations, on a good-natured tone, with examples and elements of play. The information the senior Heitzman revealed to his son was astounding. There was no way one could obtain it anywhere else, even in the most prestigious universities in the world.

"Tell me, John," asked the father, "do you know how many wealthy people there are in our country? Or in the world?"

"Their names are listed in business journals in order of their estate-value," replied John calmly.

"And where do we rank in these lists?"

This was the first time Father had used *we* instead of *I*. That meant he already considered him, John, a full partner. While he did not want to offend his father, John replied:

"Your name, Father, isn't included in these lists."

"Yes, you're right. I'm not there. Even though just our annual profit alone amounts to more than the whole estates of many included in the lists. And my name isn't there because one's wallet should not be transparent. Many of these people work either directly or indirectly for our empire — for yours and mine, son."

"Dad, you must be a genius at economics. I can't even imagine how you can make such a huge empire pay us 'tribute-money' every year without military intervention. You've managed to set up such a tremendous economic operation!"

The senior Heitzman took a pair of fire tongs and gave a poke to the logs in the hearth. Then, without a word, he poured two glasses of light wine for his son and himself. It was only after his first wee sip that he finished explaining:

"You know, I didn't set up any operation at all. The capital under my control simply allows me to give orders, and others carry them out. Many analysts and government experts in various countries, even their presidents, would be astonished to learn that the current situation in their countries is not determined by their own actions, but rather by my will.

"Political technology centres, economics institutes, analytical think tanks and government agencies in many countries — none of them are aware that they're working along strict guidelines laid down by my departments. And I don't have all that many employees. For example, all of Russia's socio-economic policy and its military doctrine are determined and controlled by one department comprising four psychologists. Each psychologist has four secretaries. Not one of them knows about the activities of the others.

"I'll tell you how the control system works — it's really quite simple. But first, John, you should understand the true laws of economics — which you'll never get from any college professor. Professors don't even know they exist. Here's a law: in the conditions of a democratic society, presidents, governments, banks, as well as major and minor entrepreneurs in all countries work for a single entrepreneur, who stands at the top of the economic pyramid. They worked for my father, now they're working for me, and soon they'll be working exclusively for you."

John Heitzman looked at his father and could scarcely take it all in. Certainly, he knew that his father was rich. But here they were talking about much more than riches — they were talking about supreme power, which was now going to be passed by inheritance to him, John. All this incredible information still had not sunk in completely. How could it be that, in a free and democratic society, everyone from presidents on down to the hundreds of thousands of firms, both major and minor — supposedly all separate legal entities — were in fact working for just one man, namely, his father?

"When I first heard from your granddad what I have just now shared with you, I had a hard time figuring it all out. Right now, John, you're probably in the same boat...

"But let me make one thing perfectly clear," the elder Heitzman went on. "There are wealthy people in this world. But for every wealthy person there is someone even wealthier. And there is one who is the wealthiest of all. All the other wealthy people — and, consequently, all the people under their control — work for him, the one who is the wealthiest of all. This is the law of the system under which we live.

"All this talk of unselfish aid to developing countries is nothing but a bluff. Sure, wealthy countries grant credit to developing countries through international funds, but in fact they do this simply to get back a healthy amount of interest in return for using their credit — in other words, to collect 'tribute-money'.

"Russia, for example, pays three billion dollars a year to the IMF, and this amount only represents the *interest* on the credit allotted to Russia. Many economists are aware that the basic financing for the IMF is provided by American capital. They realise that the extortionate interest rates on credit use is siphoned off to the USA. But who they go to specifically, nobody knows. America as a country is simply a convenient shield in the capital game. And it is dependent on capital more than any other nation. Tell me, John, did you know that America has a national debt?"

"Yes, Dad, I know. It's an astronomical figure. Just last year it amounted to... And servicing the debt cost..."

"So, that means you realise that a country which loans to other countries at the same time takes out huge loans itself?"

"Through its own Federal Reserve?"

"And who does it belong to — this Federal Reserve?"

"It... It..."

John had never thought about whom America was in debt to, but as he tried to answer his father's question it suddenly dawned on him: in the United States of America every tax-payer pays into the Federal Reserve. The Federal Reserve of the USA is a private bank. And, consequently, all America is paying hundreds of billions of dollars to private individuals... or, to a single individual.

John Heitzman had never been flustered in his life. He led, as they say, a 'healthy lifestyle'. He did not drink or smoke, he maintained a healthful diet, and worked out every day in his private gymnasium. Only in the past six months he had stopped going to the gymn. He had spent these six months ly-ing in bed in one of his spacious bedrooms, crammed full with state-of-the-art medical equipment. Doctors maintained on-call shifts around the clock in the next room.

But John Heitzman did not trust modern medical science. He felt no need of even talking with his doctors. There was one professor of psychology, however, that he occasionally deigned to favour with brief answers. Heitzman did not even care to know his doctors' names, including the name of this professor, though he did make a note to himself that he was the most sincere and honest of the lot. The professor talked a good deal, but what he said often included not just medical assertions but also reasonings and a desire to determine the causes of a disease.

One day he came in all excited and announced right at the doorway:

"I spent all last night and all this morning thinking about your condition. I think I've discovered the cause of your illness! That means that once we've removed the cause, we can talk about a pretty quick recovery... Oh, sorry, Mr Heitzman — I forgot to say hello. Good afternoon, Mr Heitzman. I got a bit carried away with my ideas."

The billionaire did not answer the professor's greeting, or even turn in his direction, but that was how he treated all his doctors. And sometimes he would make a gesture to a doctor who had just entered the room — just a slight movement with his hand, which they all knew meant: *Go away.*

Not perceiving any such gesture this time, the professor kept on explaining excitedly as follows:

"I do not agree with my colleagues on the need to transplant your liver, kidneys and heart. Granted, these organs of yours aren't functioning up to par at the moment. No sir! Not up to par! That's a fact. But neither will transplanted organs. The reason they're not up to par lies in your extreme depression. Yes sir, in your depression. I've gone over your medical history quite a few times now. And I think I've made a major discovery. Your attending physician — he's a really great guy — he wrote down everything in detail. Every single time he noted your mental condition. Your internal organs would always start to fail the moment you got into a depressive state. Yes sir! Quite a state...

"Now here comes the $64,000 question: is the failure of your internal organs causing the depression? Or the other way around: is the depression causing organ failure throughout your body? I'm absolutely convinced that the depression is the original cause. Yes sir! It's your extreme depression. It's a condition where someone ceases to strive for any goal, he loses interest in what's going on around him, he doesn't see any sense in living. And then the brain begins to transmit only half-hearted commands to the whole body! And I mean the whole of it! The stronger the depression, the weaker the commands. At a certain level the brain may cease giving these commands altogether, and then comes death.

"So, the ultimate cause is depression, and as for eliminating it entirely, well, that's something modern medicine has no answer for. So I turned to folk medicine. And now I'm convinced that your extreme depression is the result of a curse. Yes sir! More specifically, someone's put a spell on you, and I'm prepared to back that up with quite a number of facts."

The billionaire was about to make his *Go away!* gesture. He disliked all such esoteric healers — people who promised to exorcise demons and take away spells or set a defence against them — people he considered petty operators or swindlers. *No doubt the professor was on the rebound from the ineffectiveness of modern medicine,* he thought, *and so had fallen to the level of these so-called 'healers'.* But the billionaire did not manage to execute the gesture. The professor headed him off, with words evoking just a smidgen of interest, but interesting all the same.

"I have the feeling you're getting ready to send me away. Maybe for good. I ask you... No, I beg you, give me just five or six more minutes. It's very possible that once you've understood what I have to say, *you'll* make a full recovery, and

I'll make an important discovery. Rather, I've already made it — I just need to have it confirmed once and for all."

The billionaire did not make his *Go away!* gesture.

For three whole seconds the professor stared at Heitzman's motionless hand and realised he could continue, which he did at a rapid-fire pace:

"People look at each other differently. Sometimes with indifference, other times with love, or hate, or envy, or fear, or respect. But it's not the outward expression of the eyes that is the main factor here. The outward appearance can be just an ordinary mask, like the faux smile of a waiter or a salesman. What's important are the true attitudes, the true feelings one person harbours towards another. The more positive emotions people express towards a particular individual, the more positive energy is concentrated in him. On the other hand, if negative emotions predominate in the atmosphere surrounding a person, he will experience an accumulation of negative and destructive energy.

"Among the common folk this is called a *spell,* and folk-healers base their actions on this phenomenon. By no means all folk-healers are charlatans. The whole point is that a person who has been the target of too much negative energy from those around him is himself capable of neutralising it or, in other words, compensating for it. By telling the patient that he has removed the spell by certain types of actions, the healer helps him believe that he is cleansed. If the patient believes the healer, he is really evening out the balance within himself between the positive and the negative. If he doesn't believe, it won't happen. You don't believe in folk-healers and, consequently, they won't be of any help to you.

"But that isn't to say that you don't have an excess of negative energy which is destructive to your mind and body. Why negative? Precisely because a man in your position can only be looked upon by people around you with resentment, and

I don't mean just a bit of harmless envy. They might look at you — or, more specifically, treat you — with hatred. People you've fired or haven't given a raise to. A lot of people feel your power and react with fear. You see, all *that* amounts to negative energy. To counteract it you need positive energy. This can be supplied by family members or relatives, but your wives have run out on you, you don't have any children or friends, and you don't communicate with your relatives. You have no sources of positive energy around you.

"Now an individual human being is capable of producing positive energy — and in sufficient quantity — within himself, all on his own. But for this he needs to set his heart on some kind of dream or goal, and the step-by-step realisation of this goal will bring about positive emotions. You've already achieved so much in life that now, it seems, you don't have any more goals or dreams left.

"But it's extremely important to have such a goal and to strive to attain it. I have analysed the physical and mental health of different types of business people. Someone who likes mixing dough and bakes pies and sells them is happy that he can now afford to buy something he needs, and dreams of developing his business. After all, it's only with development that he receives many of the goods and services civilisation has to offer.

"A bank manager or the owner of a profit-making concern likewise strives to develop his business, strives for increased profits, but often with less enthusiasm than someone who makes or sells pies. It's paradoxical, but true — the enthusiasm just isn't as great. It isn't as great because he's got significantly fewer tempting benefits ahead of him than the pie salesman. For him the achievements of civilisation have no special value, they're just routine.

"If someone with a relatively modest income suddenly has the chance to buy a car, the purchase of the car will evoke in him a tremendous feeling of satisfaction or even ecstasy, while someone who is relatively well-off won't get any thrill from a brand new car. To him it's a mere trifle. Paradoxical, but true: rich people have fewer occasions for delight than those less well-off.

"There's one other factor that can bring satisfaction — beating one's competition. But you, Mr Heitzman, it seems, have no competition at all.

"So it turns out you have only negative energy acting upon you, and there's a great deal of it out there. Oh, and I forgot to mention: there's just one force that can conquer the masses of negative energy — just one, but it's powerful, incredibly powerful — it's called *the energy of love*. It's when you find yourself in a state of love and someone loves you. Unfortunately, in your case, however, you don't have any women in your life. In fact, it looks like you don't really have any interest in them at all, and at your age and in your condition you're not likely to have any more interest in women.

"There's a lot of evidence to back up my conclusion. I've compared the longevity stats of rich people, prominent politicians and presidents over the past hundred years. The results are quite persuasive. Longevity for the world's power brokers doesn't look all that great by comparison with the common folk — in fact, most often it's less.

"Paradoxical, but true: facts are facts. Presidents and millionaires, in spite of being under constant medical care, in spite of having access to the state-of-the-art technical help and medicines and to only the highest-quality foodstuffs, are getting sick and dying just like anyone else. All this is eloquent testimony to the fact that surrounding negative energy exerts a colossal influence, and no medical science, even the very latest, is able to counteract it.

"So, what's the bottom line? A dead-end situation? There is a way out — it may be small, it may be only one of its kind, but it's there! Yes sir! It's there. Memories!

"My dear Mr Heitzman, please, try to remember the different stages of your life. Any memory that will bring back pleasant feelings.

"Most importantly, if there's anyone you've given a serious promise to and not carried it out, see if there's any way you can carry it out now. I ask you, for your own sake, for the sake of science, to take at least two or three days and try to remember the good moments in your life. We've got equipment to monitor the functioning of many of your body organs. The monitoring goes on minute by minute. If you do what I'm recommending, and if these instruments start indicating positive results, there's indeed a chance we'll be able to see you through to a full recovery. Yes sir! You'll make it! I'll certainly find a way. Or maybe you'll find it on your own. Or maybe it'll just come about all by itself... Your life will come across it on its own."

The professor fell silent and once again fixed his gaze on the hand of his patient, lying motionless before him. A few seconds later and the customary gesture sent the professor out of the room.

Like many people, John Heitzman began to recall his past. He had at least something of an understanding of what the professor had said to him. He could try to find happy moments from his past life, and they might have a positive effect. The problem was, though, that everything he had experienced in his life seemed not just devoid of anything pleasant, it was uninteresting and even senseless.

Heitzman remembered how he took his father's advice and married the daughter of a billionaire, thereby adding to his empire's wealth. The marriage did not bring him any satisfaction, his wife turned out to be barren, and after ten years of conjugal life she died of an overdose of narcotics.

Then he married a famous fashion model, who was the very picture of a wife passionately in love. But just six months after the wedding his security service showed him snapshots of his wife cavorting with her former lover. He was not about to discuss it with her. He simply gave orders to his bodyguards to see to it that he would never have the occasion to see or be reminded about her again.

By now in his recollections Heitzman had reached the starting-point of his participation in his father's empire. He had not been able to pinpoint even one pleasant instance that he felt like holding on to and use as a source of positive emotions.

There was just one moment of pleasantness that he could remember. It was when he proved to his father that there was no need of becoming the sole owner of the Monetary Fund. Other investors in the fund, looking for a good return, would devote their mental energy to increasing the fund's capital, and thus would be working for them, for the Heitzmans.

His father took some time to think about this. Then, several days later, at dinner time, he broke with his customary reticence to offer praise and said:

"I agree with your proposal, John, regarding the Fund. You're on the right track. Congratulations! Go ahead and give some thought to other areas too. It's time for you take over the reins."

For the next several days John Heitzman was in an upbeat mood. He ended up making several more decisions and increasing the profits of their financial-industrial empire even more. However, he no longer derived any special feeling of joy from this.

The reports of increased profits were cold and dispassionate. No further praise would be coming his way. His father died, and praise from underlings brought no particular pleasure.

John Heitzman continued going back in his recollections and reached the time of his childhood. The rare moments of contact with his father were dimly illumined in his thought. His ever-strict father, as a rule, would issue admonishments in the presence of nannies and teachers which he had hired for young John.

Then all at once a wave of warmth rolled through the body of the billionaire lying motionless in his bed. His body gave a pleasant shiver. In Heitzman's recollections the curtain rose on a bright and very clear scene. He saw a far corner of the garden of his family's estate and there, surrounded by small acacia bushes, a little house about two metres high, with a single window.

For some quite inexplicable reason all children yearn to create their own little house, their own space. That yearning is there, no matter whether the child has his own room in his parents' house or lives in the same room with his parents. With almost all children there comes a time when they start building their own little cubby-hole. In every Man, apparently, there is a gene that preserves some kind of ancient memory, telling him he ought to set up his own space. Whereupon any adult or child heeding this call, which arises from the depths of eternity, goes about setting it up at once. Never mind how amateurish it turns out by comparison with modern apartments, a Man who has built this for himself derives much more satisfaction from it than he would from the most chic and stylish apartment.

And so the nine-year-old John Heitzman, who had two spacious rooms all to himself in the family manor, still decided to build his own little house with his own hands.

He constructed it out of plastic boxes that had been used for transplanting seedlings. These boxes turned out to be handy building materials. They came in a variety of colours. John made the walls using blue boxes, with a yellow border around the whole perimeter. He piled the boxes on top of each other, fastening them together in tongue-and-groove fashion. On one wall John made the box-bottoms face outward, which meant that the whole inside wall was comprised of a multitude of shelves. Boards with stapled-on plastic film served for the roof.

He spent a whole week building his little house, taking advantage of the three hours a day he was allotted for leisure walks in the fresh air. On the seventh day, just as soon as leisure time came, he headed straight for his creation in the far corner of the garden. Pulling back the acacia branches, he saw the house he had built and froze in astonishment. There by the entrance stood a little girl looking in the doorway of his creation. The girl was wearing a light-blue calf-length skirt and a white cardigan with frills on the sleeves. Her chestnut-coloured hair fell in ringlets around her shoulders.

At first, young John reacted with some jealousy to the presence of a stranger beside his creation, and he enquired with a hint of annoyance:

"What are *you* doing here?"

The girl turned her pretty little face toward him and replied:

"I'm admiring."

"What are you admiring?"

"This marvellous and clever little house."

"Wh-what kind of house?" young John queried in amazement.

"Marvellous and most clever," repeated the girl.

"Houses may be marvellous, but I've never heard them called *clever*," observed John thoughtfully. "Only people can be clever."

"Yes of course, people can be clever. But when a clever person builds a house," the girl countered, "the house turns out to be something clever, too."

"And what do you find clever about this house?"

"The inside wall is very clever. It has ever so many shelves. You can put a lot of useful things on those shelves — toys, too."

John was pleased at how this little girl reasoned things through. It flattered him, and possibly the girl herself pleased him.

She's pretty, and reasons things through cleverly, he thought to himself. And aloud he said:

"This house I built."

And he immediately added:

"What's your name?"

"I'm Sally, and I'm seven years old. I live here in the servants' quarters, since my dad works as a gardener here. He knows a lot about plants and is teaching me. I already know how to raise flowers and how to graft branches onto trees. And what's your name, and where do you live?"

"I live in the manor-house. My name's John."

"Does that mean you're the master's son?"

"Yeah."

"So, Johnnikins, let's play house!"

"How do we play that?"

"We play like we live in this house, the way grown-ups live. You can be the master, since you're the master's son, and I'll be your servant, since my dad's a servant."

"That won't work," observed John. "A servant's supposed to live in the servants' quarters. Only the husband, his wife and their children can live in the manor-house."

"Then I shall be your wife!" exclaimed Sally, and asked: "Can I be your wife, Johnnikins?"

John did not answer. He went into the house, took a glance around, and then turned to look at Sally who was still standing just outside the doorway. He said rather brusquely:

"Okay, come on in and pretend you're my wife. We have to think about how we're going to decorate the inside."

Sally stepped into the house. She looked into John's eyes with tenderness and excitement and said, almost in a whisper:

"Thank you, Johnnikins. I shall try to be a good wife to you."

John did not come to his house every day. During the time allotted for leisure walks he was not always allowed to play in the garden. Escorted by bodyguards and tutors, he would be taken instead for a visit to a city park or Disneyland, or go horseback-riding.

But when he managed to get away to his little house, he almost always found Sally waiting for him. With each succeeding visit John took interest in the changes that had been occurring in the house. First of all a carpet appeared on the floor, contributed by Sally. Then little curtains on the window and over the entrance.

Next came a little round table with an empty photo-frame on it. Sally said:

"Johnnikins, you're coming here less and less often. I keep waiting for you, but you don't show up. Give me a photograph of yourself, and I'll put it in this frame. I can look at your picture and it will make it easier waiting for you."

John left her his photograph when he came to say good-bye to the house, and to Sally. He was going to be moving with his parents to another villa.

Multibillionaire John Heitzman lay on his bed in his fancy apartment and smiled as he recalled, with ever greater detail, his childhood contact with the little girl Sally. It was only now that he realised that this little girl loved him. She loved him with her first childhood love — reckless, unanswered and sincere. Perhaps, just perhaps, he loved her, too, or perhaps she was just a passing fancy. But she loved him as probably no one else would love him the rest of his life, and so the memories attached to the little house he built in the garden and his contact with Sally still evoked in him a lot of warm and pleasant feelings. These feelings warmed his body and made him feel good.

After leaving the manor-house, he met with Sally one more time, eleven years later. But this time... New feelings excited his whole body. John Heitzman even sat up a bit in his bed. His heart had started chasing the blood through his veins with ever-increasing strength. That meeting... He had forgotten about it. He had never thought about it all this time. But now it occupied all his thoughts and made him excited.

He came back to the estate where he had spent his childhood, returning after eleven years just for a day's visit. That was all the time he could afford. After lunch he went out into the garden, and somehow he found himself heading down to the far corner of the garden, where in among the acacia bushes he had built his little house. As he pushed back the branches and stepped into the little glade, he literally froze in astonishment. The house he had built out of plastic boxes eleven years ago stood on the same spot as before. But all around... All around were little beds of flowers, and a sand-covered path led to the entrance, where a little bench was now standing. And the house itself was wreathed in flowers. The bench had not been there before, but it was there now, the grown-up John noted to himself. He pushed aside the curtain covering the entrance, bent down and stepped into the little house.

At once he could sense someone's recent presence. His childhood photo stood on the little table as before. The shelves were neatly lined with Sally's childhood toys. On one of the shelves, next to the table, stood a little bowl of fresh fruit. An air mattress lay on the floor, fitted with a coverlet.

John stood there in the little house for about twenty minutes, remembering pleasant feelings from his childhood. *Why is this happening?* he thought. His family owned a whole lot of fancy villas. There was even a castle, but neither the castle nor the villas had ever evoked such pleasant feelings as arose here, in this little house constructed of plastic seedling boxes.

When he came out of the little house, he spied Sally. She was standing there silently at the doorway, as though reluctant to interfere with the surge of recollections that had broken upon his thought. John looked at her, and noticed her cheeks flush with a rosy glow. She lowered her eyes in embarrassment, and said in a soft, velvety, extraordinarily tender and emotional voice:

"Hello, Johnnikins!"

He did not answer her right away. He stood there admiring Sally's extremely beautiful, mature body. Her figure-hugging dress fluttered in the breeze. Through the light material could be seen the outlines of her sculptured form — no longer that of a child but of a maiden, feminine and supple.

"Hi, Sally," John said, breaking a long pause. "You're still keeping house here?"

"Yes. After all, I promised. There's some fruit inside — it's just been washed. Have some. It's for you."

"I see... For me... Well, then, let's go in together and have a bite."

John pulled the curtain aside, letting Sally go ahead of him. She went in and squatted down. She took the bowl of fruit down from the shelf and placed it on the table beside the photograph in the frame.

There were no chairs in the little house, and John sat down on the rug. He reached out for a bunch of grapes and inadvertently touched Sally's shoulder. She turned her head and their eyes met. She inhaled sharply, which caused a button to come undone on the cardigan stretched taut across her breasts. John grasped hold of Sally's shoulders and drew her close to himself. She did not resist. Quite to the contrary, she leant against him with her feverishly glowing body. Sally did not resist when John slowly and carefully laid her down on the rug, or when he caressed her and kissed her lips, and her breast, or when...

Sally was a virgin... Neither before nor afterward did John enter into intimate relations with any virgin. And now, after forty years had passed since that last meeting, he, John Heitzman, suddenly realised that this had been the only really beautiful, reason-defying intimate moment he had ever had with a woman. Or, rather, with a girl, whom he had made a woman.

After that they fell asleep for a little while. When they awoke, they began talking with each other. What had they talked about? John Heitzman racked his memory as best he could. He very much wanted to remember at least part of their conversation. And he remembered.

Sally had mentioned how beautiful life was. She said her father was saving up some money to buy her a plot of land, on which, if he could afford it, he would build her a modest house. And Sally herself would do the landscape design and put in a wide variety of plants, and she would lead a happy life and raise her children there.

Back then John decided within himself that he would help Sally. *Wow,* he thought, *here's a girl that can be happy just with some plot of land and a little house. Mere trifles! I mustn't forget to help her acquire the land, and the house.*

But John did forget about his intentions. He forgot completely about Sally. He was distracted by his life with its manifold charms. A new yacht and his own private aeroplane brought joy for a few days at their first appearance. He found a longer-lasting distraction in playing the money markets, in adding billions to his father's financial holdings (which he subsequently inherited) — a distraction which excited his nerves and feelings for more than twenty years. It dominated over everything else. He went through first one marriage, then a second, as a matter of course. His wives left no trace of themselves behind. After he turned forty, playing the financial markets ceased to give him any pleasure, and he began to suffer increasingly frequent periods of depression, which finally led to a nervous breakdown.

But now John Heitzman was no longer in a state of depression. His recollections of Sally had quite stirred him up. Yet at the same time they made him angry at himself. *How could this have happened?* he thought. *I promised myself that I would help Sally, this girl who loved me, to obtain a plot of land, and a house, and I forgot.*

Now John Heitzman was a man accustomed to keeping his promises, especially those he made to himself. He realised he would never stop being angry with himself until...

He pressed a button to summon his secretary. When the secretary entered, John Heitzman was sitting on his bed. Even though he found it difficult to get out the words, for the first time in the past six months he began talking:

"Over fifty years ago I was living in a certain manorhouse — I don't remember the address, you can find it in the archives. There was a gardener working there — don't remember his name, but it's in our archived bookkeeping accounts. The gardener had a daughter, her name was Sally. Find out where Sally's living now. I need this information by tomorrow morning at the latest. If you have it earlier,

let me know at once, regardless of the hour, day or night. Do it!"

The secretary rang at dawn the next morning. As he walked into the office, John Heitzman was sitting in his wheel-chair by the window, wearing a dark-blue three-piece suit. He was shaved, and his hair neatly combed.

"Sir, the gardener was let go forty years ago and died soon afterwards. Before his death he managed to buy five acres[1] of land on an abandoned ranch in Texas. On this land he started building a house, but broke his back during the construction and died. His daughter Sally finished building the house and now lives in it. Here's the address. That's all the details we have at the moment. But on your order we'll go ahead and gather all the information you need."

John Heitzman took the piece of paper from his secretary's hand and examined it carefully. After folding it neatly, he put it into his inside jacket pocket and said:

"Have the helicopter ready for take-off in thirty minutes. It should land about four or five miles from her villa in Texas. Have a car meet me at the landing site. Just an ordinary-looking car — no limousine, no bodyguards, just the driver. Do it!"

At three o'clock in the afternoon John Heitzman, limping slightly and leaning on his cane, made his way up the gravelled path to a modest cottage surrounded by luscious greenery.

[1] 5 acres = 2 hectares approximately.

When he first spied her, her back was turned to him. The elderly woman was standing on a small stepladder, washing the outside of a window. John Heitzman stopped and stared at this woman with her beautiful ash-coloured hair. She could feel his gaze and turned to face him.

For a while she simply stood there with her eyes fixed on the old man standing on the path. Then all of a sudden she jumped down from her ladder and ran to greet him. Her step was light, and nothing about this woman looked old. She stopped about a metre from where Heitzman was standing, and in a quiet but emotional voice said:

"Hello, Johnnikins!"

Immediately she lowered her eyes and put up her hands to cover the blush on both her cheeks.

"Hello, Sally!" said John Heitzman, without another word. Or, rather, he was speaking, but only to himself, not aloud. *How beautiful you are, Sally, and how beautiful are your sparkling eyes, and the little wrinkles around your eyes! You are still just as beautiful and good as before!* Aloud he said:

"I was just passing through, Sally. I heard you were living here, so I decided to stop by. And maybe to stay the night... if I'm not imposing, that is."

"I'm so happy to see you, Johnnikins. Of course you can stay the night. I'm here alone, but tomorrow my two grand-children will be arriving for a week. I've got two of them: a granddaughter, she's nine, and a little grandson — well, he's twelve already. Come on in, Johnnikins, and I'll give you a bowl of herb tea. I know the kind of tea you need. Come on."

"So, you were married, Sally? You had children."

"I'm still married, Johnnikins," Sally answered cheerfully. "And we had one son. And now two grandchildren... Why don't you sit down at the table out there on the porch, and I'll bring the tea out to you."

John Heitzman sat down in one of the plastic armchairs on the veranda. When Sally brought out a large bowl of some kind of tea, he asked her:

"How come you said you knew what kind of tea I needed, Sally?"

"You see, my father used to gather herbs for your father. He'd dry them and then make a tea, and this tea was of great help to your father. And I learned how to gather herbs, too. My dad told me that you, too, Johnnikins, have inherited this same disease."

"But how did you know I was coming?"

"I didn't know, Johnnikins. You see, I gather them in case of any need. But tell me, Johnnikins, how are you doing? How's your life turned out?"

"In a lot of different ways, I guess. I've been busy with a variety of things, but I don't want to think about that right now. You've got a fine place here, Sally — it's beautiful, so many flowers... and a garden!"

"Yeah, it's really nice. I really like it here. But you see over there to the right, they've got a building project in the works. They're planning to build a waste treatment facility. And over to the left there'll be another factory of some sort. They're talking about moving us out...

"But you're tired from your trip, looks like you've been travelling quite a distance, Johnnikins. I can see how exhausted you are. I'll make up a bed for you by the open window. Just have a lie down and relax. Only drink up your tea first."

John Heitzman got undressed, with some difficulty. He really was tired. His muscles, atrophied by six months of lying motionless in bed, could only barely keep him on his feet. He finally managed to pull the blanket over him, and he fell asleep at once. Lately he had been unable to get to sleep at all without a sleeping pill. But here, all at once...

He slept in until noon and did not see the morning. He got up and took a shower and then went out to the veranda. Sally was getting lunch ready in the summer kitchen, and a little boy and a little girl were helping her.

"Good afternoon, Johnnikins! Looks like you got a good sleep. You look so rejuvenated! Here, meet the grandchildren. This is Emmy, and this young fella's name is George."

"And I'm John Heitzman. Good morning!" said the elderly man, extending his hand to the boy.

"So there, you're officially introduced," declared Sally. "You two go take a walk and work up an appetite while Emmy and I get lunch ready."

"I'd like to show you our garden," George said to Heitzman.

The old man and the young boy walked through the marvellous garden together. The boy kept pointing out various plants and could not stop talking about them. Heitzman, in the meantime, was concentrating on thoughts of his own. When they reached the end of the garden, the boy announced:

"Now, behind this acacia bush is my 'apartment' — Grandma made it for me."

Heitzman pulled aside a branch and looked... There in a small glade behind the acacia stood his little house — made from the same plastic seedling boxes. Only the roof looked a bit different. And the curtain covering the entrance was different. Heitzman pulled back the curtain and stooped slightly as he stepped into the little house. All the furnishings were just as he remembered them. Only the photograph on the table was laminated in plastic sheathing. The photo was of Sally's grandson. *Everything's just the way it should be,* he thought. *The little house now has a new occupant and hence a new photograph.* Heitzman picked up the photo and held it in both hands. To make conversation, he remarked:

"Well, now, little George, your photo came out pretty well here!"

"But that's not *my* photograph, Uncle John. That's a picture of a boy Grandma was friends with in childhood. It just happens he looks like me."

John Heitzman made his way back up the garden path as fast as his legs could carry him, limping with his cane, and stumbling.

Panting and feeling a little confused, he approached Sally and asked:

"Where is he now? Where's your husband, Sally? Where?"

"Please calm down, John," said Sally softly. "You shouldn't allow yourself to get so excited. Please, sit down...

"It turns out, John, that back in my childhood I promised a very fine young boy that I would become his wife..."

"But that was a game!" John Heitzman was practically shouting as he leapt up out of the chair. "A children's game!"

"Maybe so," Sally responded. "Anyway, let's say I'm still continuing to play at it. And I'm pretending that you're my husband... my husband and my beloved."

"George does look a lot like me, the way I looked as a boy. Does that mean you gave birth to a child after that night, Sally? Did you have a baby?"

"Yes, John, I had our son. And he looks like me. But he very much has your genes, and our grandson is the spitting image of *you*."

John Heitzman's gaze alternated between Sally and the boy and girl setting the table out on the veranda. He was no longer able to speak. His thoughts and feelings were confused. Then, for reasons which he himself did not fully understand, he said in a business-like tone:

"I have to leave right away. Good-bye, Sally."

He took a couple of steps down the path, then turned and headed over to Sally, who was standing there quietly. Barely supporting himself on his cane, he got down on one knee in front of her, took her hand and gave it a long, slow kiss.

"Sally, I have some very important, urgent matters to attend to. I have to leave immediately."

She put her hand on his head, softly rumpling his hair.

"Yes, of course. You have to leave, if you've got important matters and problems to take care of. If you run into any difficulties, John, you can always come here to our home. Our son now manages his own little firm — it's known by the lovely name of Lotos — and he does landscape design. He's had no special training, but I taught him myself, and he's doing some very smart designs, and there's hardly any shortage of orders. He helps me financially, and visits me every month.

"But it seems you've got some money problems? And something of a health problem, too? Come back, John. I know how to give you treatment and we've got enough money to live on."

"Thank you, Sally... Thank you... I've got to hurry! I've got to..."

He walked down the path to the gate, his thoughts all caught up in a plan he had in mind. In the meantime Sally watched John's receding figure and whispered to herself: *Come back, my love!* She was still repeating this phrase like a mantra even an hour later, forgetting about her grandchildren. She did not even notice the helicopter circling for more than half an hour overhead, over her plot of land with its little house and marvellous garden.

By the time John Heitzman's helicopter landed on the office tower roof, his close associates and their secretaries were already hard at work in the board room, feverishly checking figures, getting ready to report to the boss. They had grown unaccustomed to meeting in his presence, and now it was with considerable fear and trepidation that they awaited his arrival.

When John Heitzman entered the room, everybody rose to their feet. He began speaking even before reaching his chair at the head of the board-room table.

"Sit down. No reports today. Listen carefully to what I have to say, I'm not going to repeat myself. No time. So. In Texas there's this villa — here's the address. Your instructions are to buy up all the lands around this house within a radius of a hundred miles. Buy up all the industries located on these lands, even if it means paying three times their worth. Whichever one of you is responsible for buying and selling real estate can leave the room now and get to work immediately. Put all our agents on the job if required. This operation should take no more than one week."

One of the associates jumped up and hurried toward the exit.

John Heitzman continued:

"All buildings, factories and facilities located on these lands are to be demolished within a month, max, even if this means hiring hundreds of construction companies. A month from now grass should be planted on these sites."

Heitzman instructed the last associate remaining in the room:

"There's a firm in Texas with the pretty name of Lotos. Sign a five-year contract with it. Engage this firm to design communities for all the lands we buy up around that villa in Texas. Whatever the firm asks, double it. Do it!"

Two weeks later John Heitzman appeared before an audience of fifteen hundred people. The audience, recruited with the help of personnel firms, comprised landscape design specialists, botanists and agronomists. Everyone wanted to get work — especially since the advert mentioned the contract amount, twice the standard average.

John Heitzman walked up to the podium and began speaking in his usual authoritative tone, which was rather sharp:

"According to the contracts being offered you, each of you will receive free of charge a plot of land for lifetime use, measuring five acres. You'll be offered several designs for pre-fab homes to choose from, and these homes will be built on each plot at whatever spot you designate, all at my company's expense. For the next five years the company will make payments to each adult member of your family as specified in the contract. Your job is to make the territory you receive a place of beauty. You will plant gardens and flower-beds, and make ponds and pathways. You will make everything beautiful and good. The company will pay the cost of seedlings and whatever seed materials you request.

"That's it. If there are no questions, those who wish to accept my offer can sign their contract."

But the fifteen-hundred seat auditorium was enshrouded in utter silence. Nobody got up from their seats to head over to the tables, where secretaries were waiting with contracts ready to sign. After a minute of complete silence, an elderly man rose from his seat and asked:

"Tell me, sir, these lands where you propose we settle, are they contaminated with deadly pollutants?"

"No," replied one of Heitzman's associates. "On the contrary, this whole area has a comparatively clean environment, and the soil is quite fertile."

"Then tell us honestly," asked a young woman jumping up from her seat, "what kind of an experiment are you proposing to conduct on people? Many of us have children, and I for one do not want to subject my child to goodness-knows-what kind of an experiment."

The hall erupted with a general buzz, and cries of *Opportunists! Inhuman! Monsters!* could be heard. People started getting up and filing toward the exit. Heitzman's associates tried to explain and respond to the questions, but to no avail.

Heitzman himself sat there helplessly and watched the people leave the room. He realised that their departure was the final blow to his hopes. Or something even worse... He so wanted to do something nice for Sally, for his son and grandchildren. He wanted not only for there to be no more belching smokestacks in the vicinity of Sally's cozy cottage, but for there to be gardens around, and good neighbours too. He had bought up the lands, and the belching smokestacks had been demolished on his orders. And grass had been sown in their place. But the land could only become good if good people lived on it. And here they were leaving. They did not understand. How could they understand, anyway? What could make them believe?

Stop! All at once it dawned on him. They knew nothing about the situation, and that was why they did not believe. But now if he told them the truth... John Heitzman rose to his feet and quietly, still hesitantly, began to speak.

"People!" he began. "I understand. I need to explain to you the reasons for this action by my company. But they're impossible to explain. There's no way they can be explained. Because it's just that I... You see, it's like this... Or, rather, there's something personal to me in all these contracts. Or how shall I put it?..."

Heitzman was confused, and did not know how to continue. But the people had stopped in their tracks. They were standing in the aisles, in the exit doorways. And they were all looking intently at Heitzman. They were silent, and here he was, not knowing how to proceed. Yet somehow he managed to pull himself together and go on:

"Back in my childhood... In my youth... you see... I loved this girl. But I didn't realise back then I was in love with her. I was later married to other women. I got involved in business. For the past fifty years I never saw this girl. Never even thought about her. And then just recently I remembered her. I discovered she was the only person who ever sincerely loved me. And she still does. But I didn't know about it. Like I said, I'd forgotten all about her. And I realised that she was the only one I could ever love...

"And then... I met her. Now, of course, she's along in years. But for me she's still the same as back when I knew her years before. She loves her garden. She does everything so beautifully. And I wanted there to be beauty around her. And good neighbours. It's better for her to have good and happy neighbours living nearby.

"But how to make that happen? As a businessman I've managed to put a bit of money aside. And so I bought up the land, divided it into plots, and drew up these contracts. I did it for the one I love. Or, just maybe, I did it for myself?"

This last sentence John Heitzman uttered almost as though putting the question to himself. After that he began speaking as though talking aloud to himself, as though he did not see the people standing in front of him.

"We live for something — what do we live for? We strive for something — what is it we're striving for? I'm going to die soon — what am I leaving behind, except dust?

"But now, I'm not going to die, not until I finish my project. And I'll leave behind something eternal — I'll leave behind a garden for the one I love. I'll leave behind many gardens.

"You know, first, I wanted to simply hire a whole lot of workers and sign a contract with a big company doing land-scape design. Sign a contract so that employees could look af-ter the plants. But then it dawned on me. Any kind of beauty will turn out lifeless, if you don't create it for yourself. And that's why I decided to make it so that someone created it for themselves. That's why I'm offering you the plots of land and the houses, and all I ask in return is for beauty around the one I love.

"You didn't believe that the terms offered in these contracts were genuine. You didn't know what goals the party offering you these contracts was really pursuing. Now you know."

At this point John Heitzman fell silent. The people stand-ing in the hall were silent, too. The first to break the silence was the woman who had expressed the most scepticism ear-lier. First she hurried over to the row of tables standing by the stage with the contracts laid out, and asked one of the secre-taries to enter her name on a copy, which she signed without even reading it. Then she turned to the people standing in the auditorium and exclaimed:

"There, I've signed it. I was the first one to sign. That means I'll go down in history, because I was the first. When you think about it, not a single man, no matter how rich, has ever given a greater gift to the one he loves than this person standing there on the stage. And it would be impossible for him to do more."

"Nobody could even think of doing more," cried another woman, "in the whole recorded history of mankind!"

"I love you!" called out a third.

"I want a plot right next to your beloved," declared a fourth. "What's her name?"

"Her name..." began Heitzman, but went on: "maybe it's better she doesn't know. Let her think that this was all the will of fate."

With a single surge, the people in the hall headed over to the tables standing by the stage. A queue formed. People gaily joked with each other, calling each other simply *Neighbour,* but the majority, especially the women, kept staring at the man on the stage with sparkles of love in their eyes.

For the first time in his life John Heitzman felt the energy of good directed at him — the energy of love and unfeigned delight emanating from many human hearts. An all-triumphant energy, capable of healing any ill. He walked off the stage, now without a trace of a limp.

For several months he personally took active part in the demolition of the remaining facilities on the bought-up lands, discussed the details of design of the whole community around Sally's cottage and alternative landscape designs for different plots, along with the whole infrastructure.

A year later, when John Heitzman once again approached the gate leading to Sally's cottage, as far as the eye could see, people were already planting little saplings for their large gardens. Several saplings stood near Sally's gate, with a carefully wrapped root system. It seemed as though Sally had intuitively felt him coming, for she ran out to greet him.

"John! It's so good to see you again! Really good! Hello there, John!"

She ran up to him with a spring in her step, bubbling over like a young girl. She grasped John's arm, pulled him over to have a cup of tea, all the while happily chattering away non-stop.

"You know what's been happening, John?! You know what a miracle's been taking place here all around! I'm so superbly happy! There'll be no more belching smokestacks next to our house. There'll be good neighbours! See how life's sprucing up all around?! Really sprucing up! If you've had any business failures, John, don't worry your little head about it. You can just laugh at it and come and move in with us. We're wealthy now. Our son's just got himself a real big contract, and I mean big! He's now in charge of a whole design and planning project. And we've got ourselves a little more land. Our son's going to be building himself a new house. And the two of us, if you want to, can live here."

"I do want to," replied John Heitzman, adding: "Thank you, Sally, for the invitation."

"But why go on living in an old house?" boomed out a voice from behind John Heitzman's back. He turned around and caught sight of his son. He knew right off that it was his son. And the young man continued:

"If I understand correctly, you are actually my father?... When little George told me that you thought the photo of Mom's childhood friend was of him, I knew who'd come. And Mom never did learn to hide her true feelings.

"I, of course, don't yet have the same feelings towards you that Mom does, but for the sake of my happy parents, I am ready to pay for the building of a new house for the two of you."

"Thank you, son," said John Heitzman, almost overcome with emotion. He wanted to give his son a hug, but for some reason hesitated. The young man stepped toward him on his own, extended his hand and introduced himself:

"I'm John."

"Great!" said Sally. "And it's great now that you two have got acquainted. When you get to know each other better, you'll really like each other. But right now let's have some tea."

And as they sat at the table Sally kept on talking animatedly, non-stop, about the extraordinary events that had been taking place in the last few months.

"Can you just imagine, John? Just imagine! Here they've been telling a story like the most beautiful tale in the world. A tale which is coming true to life. Just imagine, John — people say that all these lands were bought by one and the same person. Then this person invited the best designers, agronomists and gardeners and gave each of them several acres of land free of charge for their lifetime use. He told them to make their plots beautiful. And he offered them all the saplings and seeds free of charge, and will even keep on paying them for five years to beautify their own plots. Just imagine, it is *he* who will be paying *them*. He poured all his savings into this project, right down to the last cent."

"Well, maybe not all," Heitzman protested.

"People say he put in all. And you know why he did all this?"

"Why?" asked John Heitzman calmly.

"That's the whole beauty of it. He did it so that the one he loved could have a place to live amidst all this beauty. They say she's a landscape designer as well. And somewhere around here she's got a cottage too. Only nobody knows who she is or where she lives. Can you just imagine, Johnnikins, what will happen when people find out who she is?"

"What?"

"What else? Everybody will want to go have a look at her and even touch her like a goddess. I myself, for instance, would want to touch her. She's probably an extraordinary woman. Maybe she's extraordinary outwardly, maybe inwardly. Everybody around is saying that there's no other woman in the world who could inspire a man to take such an unusual and beautiful step. That's why all the people will want to see her and even touch this man and his extraordinary wife."

"Probably they will," John Heitzman agreed, adding: "But what can we do about it, Sally?"

"What d'you mean, *we*?" Sally wondered aloud.

"I say *we*, because that extraordinary woman, the one on whose account all these things around are happening, is *you*, Sally!"

Sally stared at John without blinking, trying to make sense of what she had just heard. When the first glimpses of understanding dawned on her, she let the cup she was holding slip out of her hands, but nobody paid attention to the sound of it breaking to pieces. John Heitzman turned his head in the direction of another sound — the sound of a chair falling, when his son impulsively jumped up from his seat. The younger John rushed over to his father and said excitedly, in a soft baritone voice:

"Father! Father! Can I give you a hug?"

John Heitzman was the first to embrace his son. He could hear how his son's heart was racing. His son gave him a hug in turn, whispering excitedly:

"The world has never witnessed such a powerful declaration of love, without even using the words of love, ever! I'm proud of you, Father! I'm so happy for you, Father!"

When father and son turned to Sally, she was still trying to come to terms with what had happened. All at once her cheeks flushed with a rosy glow, as though smoothing out the wrinkles around her eyes. Tears began rolling down her cheeks. Sally was embarrassed. She rushed over to the elder John, grabbed him by the arm and led him down the front porch steps. Their son watched as his parents, hand in hand, started making their way slowly down the path, heading for the acacia bushes which concealed the little house of their childhood, and then began skipping toward the acacia like youngsters.

Ten years later a much younger-looking John Heitzman was sitting at a local café-bar with some other men from the community. He laughingly explained:

"No, I won't run for any presidential office — don't even try to tempt me. And it's not just a matter of age. You don't have to be president to run the country. That's something you can do from right in your own garden. See, you've shown by your own example how to really make a good life, and all America is now turning into a flourishing garden. If it goes on like this, heck, we'll even overtake Russia!"

"We'll do it! We'll do it" echoed Sally, who had just come in. "Only now, let's head for home, Johnnikins. The baby won't go to sleep without you." Then she added, whispering in his ear: "And neither will I."

And so they began walking home, down a shady, sweet-smelling allée, these two not-yet-old people: John Heitzman and Sally. In the springtime it always seemed that their life was just beginning. Just as real life was beginning all over America.

"That's a beautiful ending to your story," I told Anastasia, when she had finished telling her account of the future. "And all your stories are so encouraging. But will something like that really happen? In real life?"

"It will definitely happen, Vladimir. That is no made-up story, but a projection of the future. The names and locales are not important. What is important is the essence, the idea, the dream! And if my story has evoked positive feelings, then people will certainly project its essence into the future, and many people will add their own details and infuse the projection with their own great meaning and conscious awareness."

"How does all that come about?"

"See how simple it is. Did you like the story?"

"Did I like it? *I'll* say!"

"Do you want it to come true in the future?"

"Of course I do."

"What if you tell it to others? Will there be those who will want to see something like that come true, too?"

"I dare say there will."

"You see, that means that anybody will want to, who takes on the role not just of an observer of history, but an actual participant in it. And they will make the story come true."

"Yes, I think that's clear enough. But I'm just a bit sad that you went and painted such a beautiful scene in respect to foreign entrepreneurs, rather than Russians."

"Vladimir, for Russians, life is already drawing beautiful and real scenes all on its own. Or, to put it more accurately, many Russians are working out the Divine eternity. And that is something you could tell about all by yourself."

"By myself? Well, I guess so. I really do know quite a few Russian entrepreneurs who have taken not just one but several hectares of land and are building their domains on them. Like the ones you described. Only their stories aren't as romantic."

"Grand chapters need to be written about anyone who has made conscious contact with the Earth. Such a story will be inexhaustible. Look, here is just one story — see if you can recognise some familiar names."

CHAPTER EIGHT

I am giving birth to you, my angel!

Viktor Chadov, an entrepreneur, awoke at dawn. His girl-friend lay beside him in the big bed, still asleep. The thin blanket hugged the contours of her delicate figure.

Every time they attended formal receptions together or went to some fancy resort hotel, her body attracted men's envious or lustful glances.

Not only that, but Inga (as this sleeping beauty was called) possessed a most charming smile and gave the impression on those around her of being a smart and educated woman. Viktor took such great pleasure in her company that he bought a second four-bedroom flat, furnished it with ultra-modern pieces and gave Inga the keys. Occasionally, if his intensive business schedule allowed, he would spend a night or two with her. He was grateful to this twenty-five-year-old woman for these marvellous nights they spent together, and the opportunity to chat with her, but he had no plans to marry her. He had no special feelings of love for her. And, besides, he knew which side his bread was buttered on: after all, he was 38 and she 25. Naturally, it would not be long before this young woman would start hankering for a younger man. And, with *her* body and brains, that would not be too difficult to find. And she would find a younger and even richer man, all thanks to him. After all, if he married her, he would be also introducing her to a circle of influential businessmen.

Inga turned her face toward him, smiling in her sleep. The blanket had slipped down just enough to expose one of her alluring, so perfectly shaped feminine breasts. But this time

Viktor Chadov experienced none of his usual stimulation at the sight of her half-naked body. He carefully replaced the blanket on his sleeping partner. Silently, trying not to wake her, he got up from the bed and headed out to the kitchen.

He made some coffee and poured himself a cup. Lighting a cigarette, he began pacing the spacious breakfast-room floor, practically oblivious to his surroundings.

What a dream! His feelings were still aroused by last night's extraordinary dream. Yes, his *feelings,* rather than his mind. Viktor had dreamt that he was walking along a shady allée, concentrating on the feasibility of a routine commercial deal. Behind and in front of him walked his bodyguards. He was irritated at their presence and had a hard time concentrating. His attention was also distracted by the constant noise of traffic along the edge of the park.

Then all of a sudden his bodyguards disappeared and the traffic noise died down. And he could hear the birds singing, he could see the marvellous spring foliage on the trees lining the allée, and the flowers on the bushes. He stopped and delighted in the soft and pleasant feelings welling up inside him. And he felt better than he ever had before in his life.

And all at once he noticed, far down the allée, a little boy running toward him. The sunlight was shining from behind, giving him a kind of halo, and it almost seemed as though here running toward him was a little angel.

A moment later and it dawned on him that this was none other than his own little son. The lad's hands and feet were in constant energetic motion. With a joyful premonition, Viktor squatted down and threw open his arms to embrace him, while his little son, in turn, threw open his arms on the run. But then all at once the boy stopped in his tracks, about three metres shy of Viktor. The smile faded from the youngster's face, and the look in his eyes made Viktor's heart start to pound.

"Come on, come to me! Come and let me hug you, son."

The boy answered with a wry smile:

"There's no way you can do that, Papa."

"Why not?" Viktor asked in surprise.

"Because..." answered the boy with a tone of sadness. "You can't hug me, Papa, because you can't hug a son which hasn't been born. After all, you didn't give birth to me, Papa."

"Then you come and hug me, son. Come on."

"I can't hug a father who didn't give birth to me."

The boy tried to smile through his tears. A tear was already trickling down his red cheek. Then the boy turned, hung his head, and slowly wandered off down the allée.

But Viktor was still standing there on his knees, rooted to the spot. The boy kept getting further and further away. As did the soft and pleasant feeling Viktor had had a moment ago. Once again, from the distance, it seemed, he could hear the roar of traffic. Unable to move, Viktor summoned up his remaining strength and called out:

"Don't leave me! Where are you going, son?"

The youngster turned, and he could see another tear trickling down his face.

"I'm going into the nowhere, Papa. Into the infinite nowhere." Again the lad hung his head without saying a word. Then he added: "I'm sad, Papa, I'm sad that I wasn't born and so I cannot restore your life with myself."

With head lowered, the little angel receded into the distance and presently disappeared, literally dissolving in the Sun's rays.

The dream ended, but the impressions of the marvellous soft and pleasant sensations lingered on. It was as though they were summoning Viktor to take action.

After finishing his third cigarette, Viktor extinguished it firmly and decisively. He rushed into the bedroom, calling out loudly on the way:

"Wake up, Inga, wake up!"

"I'm not asleep," answered the beautiful girl from the bed. "Just lying here, lolling about. I've been wondering where you disappeared to."

"Inga, I want you to have a child. Could you have a son with me?"

She threw off the blanket and leapt out of bed. She ran over to him, flung her arms around his neck and pressed against him with every inch of her supple and beautiful body. And then in a hot whisper she confided:

"The most delightful and beautiful declaration of love is when a man asks a woman to bear his child. Thank you... that is, if you're not just joking."

"I'm not joking," he replied firmly.

Putting on a bathrobe, Inga responded:

"Well, if you're not joking — if you're serious, that is... This is a decision we need to think through. First, I want my future child to have a father. But you, my dearly beloved, are still married."

"I'll get a divorce," Viktor promised. In fact, he had already divorced his wife three months before, but for a variety of reasons had not yet told Inga the news.

"Once you get your divorce, then we can start talking about a child. But I'll tell you right off, Viktor. Even if you get divorced, it's still too early to think about children.

"In the first place," Inga reasoned — half in jest, half serious, "I still need a year to finish graduate school. Secondly, I'm so tired of studying that once I finish, I'd like to take another year just to fool around, make the rounds of a few resorts and have a good time. So, if you're talking about a child... Well, children could put an end to that little plan once and for all!"

"Okay, I was joking," Viktor interrupted her rambling train of thought. "I've gotta go. Got an important meeting coming up. I've already called for my car. So long!"

He left, but it was not for any meeting, and he had not called for any car. Viktor walked slowly down the sidewalk, giving the once-over to every woman he met. He was viewing them through new eyes — a view he himself was not accustomed to. He was trying to pick out a woman who might be worthy of bearing him a son — a woman he felt he could have a child with.

Immediately all the stylish girls with heavy makeup who had earlier attracted his attention fell away. He had completely lost interest in all the girls who dressed in tight-fitting clothes or semi-nude in mini-bikini tops to show off their figure.

It's clear why they do that — it's what's on their minds, he thought to himself. *And then they try putting an intelligent expression on their face. They use their various body parts to attract men, and maybe someone will bite. And they do bite, of course, only not to have kids. It's a bite for a shag, no procreation there. Go on, dummies, wiggle your behinds! I'm not going to let any wigglers like that have* my *child.*

Two girls he happened to notice coming toward him were smoking as they walked, and one of them was holding in her hand an open bottle of beer.

Now they're the kind that are absolutely no good for having children. Only an idiot would want to have a child with that *sort.*

Another thing Viktor noticed was that very few of the women and girls he saw were really healthy-looking. Some were slouching, others had an expression on their face that made them look as though they were suffering from stomach cramps. Still others showed definite signs of either obesity or anorexia.

No, it wouldn't do to have children with them, Viktor thought to himself. *Wow! It looks like every one of those women is dreaming of a prince sidling up to them in a white Mercedes, and yet they themselves couldn't do the most basic thing of all for that prince. In their own unhealthy state, they couldn't possibly give him a healthy child.*

Viktor did not bother to call his driver. Instead, he went on to his office on the trolleybus, still looking up and down every woman his eyes fell upon, trying to find among their number one who was worthy to bear his child, but to no avail.

All day long, including during his lunch break and when he was alone in his office, he could not stop thinking about the woman who was to give him a son.

At times he had the impression of looking for a woman he himself could be born from. At long last he came to a conclusion: if an ideal partner could not be found, she would have to be created. For this he would need to find a more or less healthy young woman with an attractive (or, at least, not a repulsive) appearance, one with a good character, and arrange for her to have all sorts of training and health-improvement exercises in the best sanatoriums. But the main thing would be to send her off to be tutored in a top educational institution, one where she could learn all about preparing for pregnancy, carrying the child to term and the birthing process itself, as well as basic pre-school education.

At the end of his working day, he called in his firm's lawyer, Valentina Petrovna, a woman who had been made wiser by the school of hard knocks.

He invited her to have a seat and began in a roundabout way:

"I have a bit of an unusual question for you, Valentina Petrovna. It's rather personal, but it's very important to me. A cousin of mine asked me to make an enquiry for her. Anyway, she's planning on getting married soon, and she asked me to find out where she can locate an educational institution in our country for women to study up on the best way to carry their pregnancy, as well as what the birth process and subsequent child-raising involves. And what the role of the father should be in this."

Valentina Petrovna listened intently. When he finished, she thought for a while before saying:

"As you know, Viktor Nikolaevich,[1] I have two children, and I've always been interested in literature on birthing and the raising of children, but I've never even heard of that kind of school, either in our country or abroad."

"Strange! They teach everything nowadays, and yet this most important issue isn't touched in either our high schools or our post-secondary institutions. I wonder why?"

"Yes, it *is* strange," Valentina Petrovna agreed. "I've never really thought about it before, but now this state of affairs does seem strange to me. The State Duma, it looks like, doesn't shy away from discussing the topic of sex education in the schools, but the question of teaching how to give birth to and bring up children isn't even raised."

"That means that every couple is obliged to experiment on their own child?"

"That's what it boils down to," replied Valentina Petrovna. "An experiment. There are, of course, a wide variety of courses teaching parents what to do at birthing time, how to handle newborns, but there's no scientific basis underlying the process, and it's pretty nigh impossible to decide which courses are really going to help and which are harmful."

"Did you take any courses yourself, Valentina Petrovna?"

[1]*Petrovna, Nikolaevich* — These are patronymics. See footnote 9 in Book 1, Chapter 1: "The ringing cedar".

"Well, for our younger daughter I decided on a home birth, in the bathtub, with the help of a midwife. A lot of women are doing that today. People believe that it's more comfortable for a child to make its appearance in the world in a home environment, in the presence of family. They say newborns can tell when people treat them with love as opposed to just simply indifference, which is what you get in many maternity wards. It's like a conveyor belt there, after all."

Viktor did not find his conversation with Valentina Petrovna all that encouraging. In fact, it depressed him. For two whole weeks he spent all his free time thinking about the problem of childbirth. For two whole weeks, as he walked about the city on foot, visiting high-class restaurants, bars and theatres, he would give probing looks into women's faces. He even went out into the countryside, but could not find anyone suitable for him there either.

One day he parked his jeep near a teacher's college and peered through the jeep's tinted glass windows at the girls passing by. After three hours he noticed a young woman coming down the steps with her hair tied back in a short, light-brown braid. She had a stately figure and, as it seemed to him, an intelligent-looking face. As she walked past his jeep on the way to the bus stop, Viktor rolled down his window and hailed her:

"Excuse me, please, miss. You see, I've been waiting for my friend here, and I can't wait any longer. If you could show me the best route to the centre of town, I'd be happy to give you a lift home after that, if you like."

The girl looked at the jeep, assessing the situation, and then quietly answered:

"Sure, why not? I'll show you."

After she got into the front seat and they had introduced themselves, the girl pointed to the pack of cigarettes on the dashboard and said:

"You got some nice cigarettes there. Mind if I have a smoke?"

"Help yourself," replied Viktor. He was just as glad when his mobile phone rang at that moment. No important message, but when he hung up, Viktor put on a worried face and told the girl, who by now was aggressively puffing on a cigarette:

"Something's come up. I've gotta get to an urgent business meeting. You'll have to excuse me."

With that he let the girl out on the sidewalk, cigarette in hand, after deciding there was no way he was going to let his son be poisoned by tobacco smoke.

All during these two weeks Viktor did not meet with his girl-friend at all. He did not even ring her up. He had decided that if she did not want to have a child with him, if all she wanted to do was have a good time and hang around fancy resorts, he had no use for her.

Certainly, it had been fun spending time with this beauti-ful and intelligent woman, but now his life-plans had taken a completely different turn. *I'll leave her the flat,* Viktor de-cided. *After all, this woman did spice up my life for a while.* He headed over to the university Inga attended, to give her his keys to the apartment. On the way there he rang her up on his mobile:

"Hi, Inga!"

"Hi!" came the familiar voice over the telephone. "Where are you now?"

"I'm almost at your university. Will you be finished classes soon?"

"I haven't gone to the university for ten days now. To tell you the truth, I can't see myself going back there any time soon."

"Something happened?"

"Yeah."

"Where are you now?"

"At home."

When Viktor opened the front door and entered the flat, Inga was lying on the bed in her bathrobe and reading some kind of book. Glancing at Viktor, she said, without getting up:

"There's coffee and sandwiches in the kitchen."

And once more she buried her nose in her book.

Viktor went into the kitchen and took a couple of gulps of coffee. After lighting a cigarette, he plunked his keys down on the kitchen table, then went back to the door of the bedroom, where Inga was still reading, as before.

"I'm leaving," he told her. "Maybe for quite a while, or maybe for good. I'm leaving you the flat. Good-bye. Take care of yourself, hang loose."

And with that he headed toward the door. Inga caught up with him right in the doorway.

"Hey, wait a minute, there, scamp!" she said with an upbeat tone, tugging at Viktor's sleeve. "You're leaving me, eh? You turn my whole life upside-down, and now it's 'Good-bye'?"

"Now how have I turned your life upside-down?" Viktor asked in surprise. "You gave me a good time, and I bet it wasn't too bad for you either. You now have the flat all to yourself, and a closet full of clothes. Take care of yourself, have fun the way you wanted to. Or is it more money you want?"

"You know, you really *are* a scamp! C'mon! First you spit on my soul, and then you carry on about the flat, clothes, having fun?"

"Hey, take it easy. Don't make a scene. I've got important business to attend to. Good-bye!"

Viktor reached for the door handle. But Inga once again held him back, grabbing hold of his arm."

"Not so fast, darling. Hold on a moment. There's something I want you to tell me. Did you ask me to bear a child, or didn't you?"

"I asked, and you said no."

"Yeah, I said no, at first. Then I thought about it for a couple of days and changed my mind. I quit graduate school, quit smoking, I work out every morning, and now I've got hold of these books about life, and children. I can't put them down. Here I am reading up on the best way to have a child, and he says 'Good-bye'! I can't imagine anyone but you as the father of our..."

When Inga's words finally sunk in, Viktor gave her a boisterous hug, whispering her name over and over again. Then he hoisted her in his arms and carried her into the bedroom. Tenderly, as though handling a most precious treasure, he laid her down on the bed and began tearing off his clothes. With greater passion than ever before he embraced her as she lay on the bed. He began kissing her shoulders and breast, at the same time trying to remove her bathrobe. But all at once his efforts met with a silent protest, and she started to push him away.

"Hey, calm down there... please!" Inga said to him. "That's not the way. To put it in a nutshell, I'm not going to have sex with you today. Or tomorrow, or a month from now."

"What d'you mean, no sex? Didn't you just tell me you agreed to have a child?"

"That's what I said."

"But how can you have a child without sex?"

"Sex should be something quite different. Fundamentally different."

"How so?"

"Well, it's like this. Tell me, my dear, future, loving Papa, why do you want your child to be born?"

"What are you talking about?" Viktor sat down on the bed in shock. "Everybody knows why. There's no two ways about it."

"You're making yourself very clear. But still, let's be specific as to what you want and which way you want to go about it. D'you want your child to be born as a consequence — a side-effect — of your fleshly desires? Or of our joint fleshly desires, for that matter? Or would you rather see him as the desired offspring of our mutual love?"

"I don't think a child would fancy being just a side-effect."

"So, then, the offspring of love. But, you see, you're not in love with me. Sure, you find me attractive, but that's not the same as love."

"You're right, Inga, I find you *very* attractive."

"There, you see? And you're very attractive to me, but that's still a ways from love. We have to earn each other's love."

"You must have been hitting some pretty strange reading material, eh, Inga? Love is a feeling, it comes all by itself from goodness-knows-where. And it disappears goodness-knows-where. You can earn somebody's *respect,* sure, but love?..."

"But it is precisely each other's love that we've got to earn, and our son will help us do it."

"Our son?! You really feel we're going to have a son?"

"Why 'going to'? It's already a fact."

"Hey, what does that mean?" Viktor jumped up. "Are you telling me you're already pregnant? You've been hiding it from me, eh? Whose child is it? How far along is it?"

"It's yours. And it hasn't started yet."

"So, it's not there yet at all?"

"It is."

"Listen here, Inga. I really have no idea what you're on about. You're talking some sort of nonsense. Can't you put it, somehow, more clearly?"

"I'll try. You see, Viktor, you got this desire to have a child and you've begun thinking about it. Then I got the same desire, and I too began thinking about it. We know today that human thought is material. And that means, if we both have a mental concept of our child, it already exists."

"And where is it now?"

"I don't know. Maybe in some other dimension we don't know about. Maybe, out there in some one of the galaxies of the Universe he's running barefoot through the stars and looking down on this blue Earth where he's going to get a material embodiment. Maybe he's now choosing the place and conditions he'd like to be born in, and wants to let us know. Can't you hear, or feel, what he's asking us?"

Viktor looked at Inga wide-eyed, as though seeing her for the very first time. She had never come out with reasoning like this before. He could not make up his mind whether she was serious or simply joking. But that phrase *maybe he's now choosing where he'd like to be born* stuck in his mind.

People are born in all sorts of different places — some are born in an aeroplane, on board ship or in a motor car. Many are born in hospitals in maternity wards, some at home in the bathtub. They are born wherever it works out for them to be born, but where would children *like* to be born? For example, he, Viktor, if he had had the opportunity and the choice, where would he like to have been born? In Russia, or in one of the best hospitals in England or America? But none of these alternatives struck him as being particularly appealing.

Inga interrupted Viktor's train of thought:

"I've already worked out a detailed plan for our joint preparation for meeting our son."

"What sort of plan?"

"Listen to me carefully, my dear." Inga spoke decisively like never before, either sitting in an easy chair or pacing the floor. "First, we've got to get ourselves in top-notch physical shape. From now on we shan't smoke or drink. We have to do a thorough cleaning out of our insides, starting with the kidneys and liver, with the help of various teas and fasting. I've already selected a method.

"From now on we shall drink only spring water — that's very important. I'm already having five litres of spring water delivered every day. Sure, it costs twice as much as in the stores, but never mind, we'll get by.

"Every day we need to do physical exercises to strengthen our muscles and intensify our blood circulation. We still need fresh air and positive emotions, which are not all that easy to come by."

Viktor liked Inga's decisiveness, as well as her plan of action. Without giving her a chance to finish, he declared:

"We'll buy the best work-out equipment for our physical exercises, and hire the best masseurs. I can send one of my drivers to pick up spring water for us every day. The driver can also go and collect air from the forest — he can use a compressor to store it in cylinders under pressure, and then we can release the air in our flat a little at a time. Only I have no idea where we can get or buy positive emotions. Maybe we could go visit some fine resorts, like on our honeymoon trip? I mean it — *a honeymoon.*"

Viktor's mood was getting more and more upbeat by the minute — thanks both to Inga's decisive and carefully thought-through approach to childbirth and to her desire to have a child by him. And he was glad to know that the son he had foreseen in his dream would be borne not by just some flighty female interested mainly in money but by Inga, who was taking such a serious and responsible approach to the matter.

He really wanted to do something nice for Inga, whom he already considered to be the mother of his future son! He got up, quickly put on a suit, walked up to Inga and solemnly declared:

"Inga, will you marry me?!"

"Of course I will," Inga replied in accord, as she buttoned up her bathrobe. "Our son should have official parents. Only there's no point in going to some fancy resort for our honeymoon — that doesn't fit in with my plan of preparation for childbirth."

"What does fit in, then? Where else can we get positive emotions?"

"We should go around the outlying villages and find a spot we both really like. It has to appeal to both of us, and that means it will appeal to our son too, when he sees it. We'll buy a hectare of land there, and you will build a small house where our child's conception is to take place. I shall stay there all nine months of my pregnancy, maybe with an occasional brief outing. We'll plant a new garden right there on our very own plot of land. I shan't give birth in a hospital, but in the little house on our family domain."

Viktor could not believe his ears. He could not believe that Inga — a smart, glamorous woman who used to be so keen on hanging out at fashionable clubs and popular resorts — could have changed her whole way of life so radically. On the one hand, he was flattered by Inga's vision — after all, she had *his* child in mind. On the other hand, did not this vision harbour just a hint of abnormality?

He had heard from one of his friends of the existence of a series of books describing an unusual approach to childbirth. His friend had mentioned the importance of each family having their own hectare of land, and had given him this little book with a green cover called *The Book of Kin*. He had not got round to reading it, but he had heard that these books had been stirring up quite a controversy among the public. People who read them were beginning to change their whole way of life.

All at once, Viktor's eyes fell on a pile of books with green covers lying on one of the bedside tables. He walked over and read the series title: *Ringing Cedars of Russia.*[2] Among them was *The Book of Kin*. Viktor now realised that all these unusual ideas Inga had about preparation for childbirth she had taken from these books, and she was getting ready to carry them out to the letter. He was still not quite sure whether this was a good or a bad thing.

There was something disturbing about Inga's unusual and unquestioning conviction. It was as though an invisible someone had changed her views and whole outlook on life. But had these books changed Inga for the better, or had they made her just a little quirky? Viktor kept rehashing the question over and over in his mind, and began to argue with her:

"Inga, I know you got your ideas from these books. I've heard about them. Some people find them exciting, others say there's a lot in them that's simply fairy-tale-ish and can't be proved. Maybe you shouldn't just automatically believe everything that's in them? Think about it — what's the point in our taking a plot of land and building a little house and wearing ourselves out planting trees?

"I've got enough to buy us a fine mansion with landscaped grounds, a swimming pool, nice lawns, pathways and a garden, if that's what you want."

"There's a lot of things we could buy, of course," Inga blurted out, very emotionally, for some reason, "even a facsimile of love. But I want us to plant our garden ourselves. All by ourselves! 'Cause I want to be able to say to my son when he grows up: *You see this apple tree, son, and that pear tree and the cherry tree? I planted and watered them myself when you were just a little tyke. I did that for you. You were oh so little, and these trees were oh so little. Now you've grown, and they've grown too, and they've begun to bear fruit for you. And I've tried to make the whole Space around your little Motherland nice and beautiful for you.*"

Inga's outpouring of emotion was convincing, and Viktor liked what he heard. He even started having regrets that nobody in his lifetime had been able to take him to a garden like that and say: "This tree here was planted and grown for you by your parents." *Yes, of course, Inga's right,* thought Viktor, *only why is she talking only about herself, as if I don't exist?* Feeling a bit slighted, he asked:

"Inga, why would you tell our growing son only about *your* part in this?"

"'Cause you don't want to plant a garden," Inga calmly replied.

"What d'you mean, I don't want to? You bet I do, if it's important for our future."

"Well, then, if we're going to do everything together, I'll tell our son *we* planted this garden for him."

"That's more like it," Viktor observed, comforted.

For two months Viktor and Inga spent all their weekends driving around the outskirts of the city, looking for a place to build their future kin's domain. It was a most pleasant undertaking, and right at that time it seemed to Viktor that there was no more important task in life than searching for the one place on the Earth that would satisfy his soul and, consequently, that of his future son.

And so it happened one day that they came to the edge of a deserted village about thirty kilometres outside the city.

"There it is," Inga said quietly, jumping out of the car first.

"I feel something here, too," responded Viktor.

Later they made a second trip to the place, and spent a whole day looking over the site and talking with the local residents. They were told that the soil was not all that fertile, as there was ground water fairly near the surface. But that did not faze Viktor. He became more and more persuaded that this particular land, along with the little birches growing on it, as well as the sky and clouds above it — that all of this belonged to him. To him and his future son, and to his and Inga's grandchildren and great-grandchildren. And if the ground was not all that fertile, no matter — he would make it fertile.

It did not take long to draw up the documents to purchase two hectares of land, and after four short months the plot sported its own pretty, almost fairy-tale cabin, built of kiln-dried logs.

The cabin featured a sauna and a biotoilet, along with hot and cold running water straight from a well dug on the spot. And on the second floor — a cozy bedroom with a window overlooking a forest and a lake.

Inga designed the layout of the cabin with all its furnishings. She also came up with a plan for the landscaping. Together they planted cedars, firs and pines around the perimeter of the lot, as well as little fruit-tree saplings. Every evening Viktor would hurry home to his little cabin on his future domain, where the mother-to-be of his child was taking care of the home front.

All the women Viktor had known before not only receded into the background — they simply ceased to exist for him at all. Inga's radical approach to childbirth engendered new feelings in him. They were still not entirely clear to him, and they were probably quite different from traditional love, but he was quite convinced that he could never part from her, and only she could bear...

It was only with her that he could build a future. The two of them went in to Moscow together to attend courses on home childbirths. There was one peculiarity of Inga's that Viktor found disconcerting — her outright refusal to have intimate relations with him. She kept insisting that their child should not be born as a result of fleshly lusts, but from Man's infinitely greater and more meaningful desire, which was something else again.

Now this time the author of these little green books has gone too far! thought Viktor. *Come on, could it really be possible to do away with the factor of fleshly desire completely?*

But one day, as he lay beside Inga on the bed, not having any kind of sex in mind but thinking only of his future son, he touched her breasts. Inga at once pressed against him and put her arms around him...

In the morning, while Inga was still asleep, Viktor headed over to the lake. The world around him seemed entirely different — it seemed unusual and joyful.

What had happened the previous night he had never experienced before, either with Inga or with any of the other women he had known. This was no ordinary sex. It was an inspired impulse of creativity. Of course people are born and people die. But if they never experience anything like this over their whole lifetime, they are missing something — maybe the most important thing. But thanks to Inga, it did not escape Viktor. And he began to experience new warm — yea, fervent — feelings toward the one woman in his life: Inga.

All nine months of her pregnancy Inga spent on the domain, going into town only occasionally. She had it all worked out where the baby pram would be kept and where the crib would stand. She even had Viktor plant a modest-sized lawn where she could walk with their little son.

Her contractions began a week ahead of the expected time. Their future son was apparently anxious to make his appearance in his marvellous Space on the Earth.

From the information they had received during their childbirth courses, Viktor knew what a father should do to assist during the labour, but the only rational thing he turned out to be capable of accomplishing was to ring up the midwife they knew and call for an ambulance to stand by in case of emergency. Inga had to draw the water in the bathtub herself, prepare the towel and measure the water temperature, while he paced the room trying to think what he should be doing, but could not for the life of him recall what it was.

With no husbandly help to count on, Inga climbed into the bathtub on her own. The contractions continued, but each time one occurred, she simply drew upon her beautiful voice to sound forth on notes of joy and triumph.

Finally, out of all he had learnt during the courses, Viktor managed to remember one thing: *positive emotions.* He glanced over at the windowsill and saw the flower Inga had planted in a pot there — now in full bloom. He grabbed the flower-pot and ran with it into the bathroom, exclaiming excitedly over and over again:

"Look, Inga, your flower's blooming! Your flower's blooming! It's come out, just look!"

He was standing there holding the flower-pot when his son's little body appeared in the bathtub.

The midwife arrived only after Inga had already placed the tiny body on her tummy. Seeing Viktor standing there holding the flower-pot, she snapped:

"And just what are you doing?"

"I'm giving birth to a son," replied Viktor.

"Ah," the midwife nodded in agreement. "Then put your pot back on the windowsill and bring me..."

I need to tell all men... thought Viktor, as he ran about the house for the umpteenth time, *true and lasting love comes only when together with your beloved you give birth to a long-desired child.*

CHAPTER NINE

A fine state of affairs!

A fine state of affairs! We live out our lives, and we don't even try to figure out what our society's all about! And yet it is one of the most important questions in life. It's one that's troubled me for a long time now. I really wanted Anastasia to have a look at the documents on the building of the domains which I had brought with me, along with my appeal to the President of Russia and the draft legislation drawn up by my readers.

After thinking it over, however, I decided not to show these documents to Anastasia. I didn't want to risk upsetting her. Especially now, if it turns out she's pregnant, she needs positive, and not negative, emotions.

I finally decided to give the whole packet of documents to Anastasia's grandfather and asked him for his opinion.

"Oho!" exclaimed Grandfather, as he took the voluminous packet from my outstretched hands and remarked: "What d'you want me to do, Vladimir — read all this?"

"Yeah, I want to hear your opinion about them — about how things have turned out."

"And what good would that do you?"

"It would help me decide what course of action to follow."

"You ought to be deciding your own course of action, without any kind of advice."

"Does that mean you're not willing to read these?"

"All right, I'll read them, just so you won't take offence."

"I shan't take offence. What sense is there in reading if you're obviously reluctant to do so?"

"Sense? The sense is in not wasting time on useless stuff."

Grandfather sat down on the ground beneath the cedar, opened the folder and began leafing through the pages, taking his time. Occasionally his gaze would pause and focus on a particular page. Sometimes he just kept turning the pages with a passing glance. After a while he said:

"Vladimir, I need to look at everything carefully. Why don't you go take a walk in the meantime?"

I walked about twenty metres off and began pacing back and forth, waiting for him to finish reading the documents I had brought with me (including the articles prepared for the almanac).[1] I would like to share these with you too, dear readers.

Talking with presidents

Please tell me, esteemed sirs — all you presidents, prime ministers and chancellors — who in fact is in control of nation-states?

The question may seem strange at first glance. Any schoolchild will offer the reply:

"Countries are under the control of the president, the government, the Duma."[2]

But an answer like that simply points to the extent of the mass illusion at work here, and not just in our country. All

---

[1] *the almanac* — see footnote 1 in Book 7, Chapter 28: "To the readers of the Ringing Cedars Series".

[2] *Duma* — the lower house of the Russian parliament (see next chapter).

sorts of ordinary people are under the spell of this illusion, just like the rulers themselves. It can and must be dispelled with the aid of logical thinking. Those who are unable to discern the illusoriness engendered upon the Earth will die without having really lived, because the whole of their so-called life is but an illusion.

And so — how to dispel this illusion?! First of all we should define what it means to 'control a nation'. In the main, and perhaps exclusively, this refers to the control of social processes and phenomena. The chief person in this control system is called a president.

So, let's ask him:

"Tell us, please, Mr President, are you in charge of drug addiction in our country?"

"No," the president will reply. "I'm not in charge of that."

"What about the rapid development of prostitution?"

"No, I'm not in charge of that either."

"And what about widespread corruption and bribery?"

"No."

"And the extinction of our population?"

"What are you talking about? I'm not in charge of anybody's extinction."

There are a whole lot of questions which he would have to answer with the phrase "No, I'm not in charge of it." He has, in fact, no alternative, since giving any other answer would brand the ruler a criminal.

So it turns out that there are unmistakable large-scale processes taking place in society, influencing the lives of every single individual, but the supreme ruler and the whole host of officials under his command have nothing to do with these processes. *What, then, are they, in fact, in charge of?*

Upon closer inspection, all they do, it turns out, is involuntarily and unwittingly supervise the concealment of the true rulers, who, you see, really do have a reason to hide.

In any case, no president, chancellor or prime minister can possibly be the real ruler of a nation, either in theory or in practice. Their only task is to carry out someone else's will under the guise of their own, and this can be attested by scholars — psychologists, for example.

You and I can come to a similar conclusion if we make a careful analysis of our own lives.

Haven't our own lives been influenced by 'someone' — say, in kindergarten, school or college? If they want to, they can bring us up to be communists, or fascists, or democrats, as in our present situation.

And through this process of upbringing and indoctrination, they engender the corresponding social processes.

"Reality should be determined only through one's own self," Anastasia has said. Her words are good, and true. But to understand reality, we need to reflect, contemplate. However, our prevalent way of life leaves precious little time for reflection, and so by default we use someone else's definition of reality that has been imposed on us.

In the case of a head of state, he has even less time for reflection than ordinary people. His daily schedule is calculated down to the hour and minute, and often not by himself.

History also teaches us the impossibility of a universally visible ruler actually controlling a nation-state.

It is known, for example, that in Ancient Egypt the pharaoh was raised by priests. Naturally, they knew in advance what many of the pharaoh's future decisions would be. But even during the tenure of his reign they would still keep giving him advice. So in actual fact, the pharaoh was merely carrying out somebody else's will.

Rulers in the Orient also had wise-men at their courts and consulted with them. But neither the Egyptian priests nor the Oriental court wise-men, nor the sages of our Vedruss period, ever burdened themselves with affairs of state. Their principal task was that of analysis and reflection.

Not affording such an opportunity to our present rulers and parliamentarians renders them incapable of exerting an effective influence on the processes taking place in society. It deprives them of power.

This was confirmed to me by a well-known three-term deputy of the legislative assembly, who is also a professor with a Ph.D. in economics. But he confirmed this only after serving his parliamentary terms, when he finally had the opportunity to engage in reflection and analysis.

It was confirmed in the scandalous incident reported in the press when a deputy of the present Duma complained to the Constitutional Court that the President's Deputy Chief of Staff advised a group of State Duma representatives in no uncertain terms not to reason things through but simply to vote as they were told.

Incredible as it may seem, the Deputy Chief of Staff, perhaps intuitively, turned out to be the closest of all to the truth. It was far quicker and more efficient for him to make decisions on his own than to have a crowd of people beating their brains out over these decisions — a crowd of people who didn't have the opportunity to think. This conclusion is confirmed by the fact that none of the parties in the State Duma have put forward even a slightly articulate platform that the public can understand.

The situation with the ideas and programme already put forward by Anastasia offer the clearest evidence of the inability of the existing system to engage in independent decision-making.

Anastasia's programme has been supported by a great many people, and, as studies have shown, the overwhelming majority of these people lead a sober lifestyle and are inclined to reflection. Vast numbers of people in different parts of the country have overcome great challenges in their efforts to implement this programme. On the government level, however, there are people who seem incapable of even seeing what is going on in the public arena.

Not only that, but counteraction has begun which has served to highlight precisely the influence foreign powers have been exerting on Russia, and the fact that the country is far from being under the control of its own government.

This counteraction, of course, does not come from the ranks of the priests, who plan out programmes for centuries and millennia to come. It is simpler and more specific, and arises from the current system of world order, in which Russia has been assigned to the role of a supplier of raw materials for the West and a market for its substandard merchandise.

By 'the West' I do not mean the ordinary people of Europe or America. I'm talking about a group of transnational companies and financiers who are interested in their own profits.

As we can all attest for ourselves, over the past decades their plans have been implemented at an alarming rate, while our rulers, to say the least, have done nothing to prevent this implementation. This is another fact clearly testifying to their lack of any kind of true power or authority.

The only counteraction to the destruction of the state and the annihilation of a significant part of its population is the programme put forward by Anastasia.

"But," the majority of my readers might reasonably argue, "why do you continue to appeal to those who have no power and are incapable of changing anything?" I shall respond.

1. I am appealing, after all, not only to the authorities, but in the first instance to *you*, dear readers, in the hope that our combined efforts will enable us to understand the situation we find ourselves in — in the hope that this situation will come out in your interpretation in family chronicles. This is an absolutely vital step. Otherwise not only we, but our children, too, will have an unenviable future to look forward to.

2. I remember Anastasia's question: "But who is to blame for the lack of acceptance of truth — the one who does not accept the truth or the one from whom he receives it?"[3] I think that I am partly to blame for the lack of sufficient governmental support offered to those who have begun to set up their domains. I was not able to express the idea in a language government officials could understand. Sure, we all speak the same Russian language, but different segments of the population use it differently, and attach different interpretations to words.

In short, I am unable to express myself in a language government officials understand.

The President's administration, the Government and the Duma are all comprised of people, just like you and me. They too have children, wives and grandchildren, for whom, as would any other parent, they wish a bright future. And if they should prove capable of understanding the situation, they will gain true power and will be in a position to significantly influence the positive processes taking place in our society. But where and how can we find the words capable of putting an end to this "vanity of vanities"?[4] We must look! Otherwise new politicians will appear and will come up against the same system blocking their thought. Hence I am appealing to you, my readers, with a request to find together the words which will be understood by the various segments of our society.

And so for the umpteenth time, I stand my ground and appeal to our President and Government.

[3] Quoted from Book 2, Chapter 7: "Who's to blame?".
[4] *Vanity of vanities* — a quote from Ecclesiastes 1: 2.

TO THE PRESIDENT AND GOVERNMENT OF
THE RUSSIAN FEDERATION

As supreme ruler of the Russian State, you are undoubtedly more interested than anyone else in the prosperity of our country. Like any head of state, you would like to be recognised by the public for having left the brightest of all possible legacies during your tenure in office — namely, laying a foundation for the prosperity of our nation and its people.

Similarly, every Russian family desires to shape its life and daily routine in a manner worthy of human existence. And every mother who bears a child dreams about a happy future for her offspring, realising that such a future is possible only when the nation as a whole is heading in a clear and predictably good direction.

It is on this premise that you are endeavouring to build our national institutions — our government, our ministries and our regional authorities. Nevertheless, no matter how sincere your desires and the endeavours of our state apparatus may be, our country continues to be plagued by corruption, drug addiction, prostitution, juvenile crime and many other social ills.

Our environmental and demographic situation is becoming hopelessly entangled. Families are falling apart. The country's overall population is in daily decline. We as a people are simply dying out.

Everything you are doing is extremely important: the consolidation of the vertical power structure, the reorganisation of the state apparatus, the reform of the military, the doubling of the GDP in the economic sector. All our national indicators are on the plus side, the dynamics are positive, but... the public doesn't feel it. The people of our country — our neighbours, colleagues and co-workers, relatives, parents and

children — are all finding it more and more difficult to understand each other, to find kind and sympathetic words to say
to each other, to build their mutual relationships on the basis
of honesty, decency and trust. Fear for tomorrow, for the future of their children, shows no signs of letting up. Are not
these the most important indicators to consider?

We see signs of an increasingly active struggle against social ills, but these ills are not abating. Why not? Why do the
people's desires and the President's endeavours not correspond with what is happening on the ground?

Isn't it time we all faced the truth squarely in the eye and
came to the conclusion that we are struggling merely with
effects, and not with their underlying causes? Isn't it time
for you to openly admit that our country is playing host to
an ideology foreign to our society, and realise that there are
certain definite forces underlying many of our ongoing social
ills? As a professional KGB man, you couldn't help but be
aware of this.

These forces have made such fools of our peoples that we
are beginning to suffer from tunnel vision. Take a simple example: *advertising.* Both learned psychoanalysts and ordinary
people will tell you that mass advertising is nothing but a device which exerts a powerful influence on the human psyche.
With the aid of this device people in many countries can be
persuaded to consume food products which are harmful to
their health, or wear uncomfortable clothing, or vote for certain politicians. And this device, which can exert a colossal
influence on masses of people, seems to be in your hands, in
the hands of our national government. Isn't that so?

Most definitely *not*! It is actually subject to *other* masters.
Attempts to bring resolution to this question immediately
give rise to accusations of violating freedom of speech. These
accusations come from those who actually have no interest
whatsoever in promoting people's freedom of speech. The

mass media are, in fact, in the hands of the world's financial magnates.

And they keep spreading this monstrous lie among whole populations, hiding behind the cynical excuse that it is advertisers who support all TV and all the interesting programmes we "so love to watch". But, in fact, TV is not paid for by any advertisers. All they do is pass on a portion of the money they collect from the public, which they build into the cost of their products in order to pay for their advertising on TV, radio, public transport and the street. Thus it turns out that the public collectively are the real supporters of TV operations — every time they purchase substandard consumer goods and food products containing chemical additives. They support mediocre and downright shoddy TV programmes and soap operas, which keep promoting the image of Man as a maniacally preoccupied Neanderthal.

The science of imagery, and who governs the country's ideology

Throughout history national ideologies have been created through devices which exert an influence on human society through images, through the clandestine ancient knowledge of the science of imagery.[5] Some of our learned chaps might object that there is no such science. But there is. And its

---

[5]For further references to the science of imagery, see Books 4, 6 and 7, especially Book 6, Chapter 6: "Imagery and trial".

existence is determined not by the will of academics, but by the very nature of Man. Man is created to think, and thoughts in turn form images.

In recent times we are wont to associate the science of imagery with Ancient Egypt. We learn from history how priests created images to liberate nation-states or seize power over whole peoples.

It was the same kind of knowledge that the SS troops attempted to master in Hitler's Germany, or the KGB's Division 13 in Soviet times.[6]

Certain elements of this science are intuitively employed by modern political technologists in the West, and more recently in our own country. Hence the terminology *image-making, way of life, way of thinking,*[7] *a candidate's image.*

To the political technologists it is quite unimportant what a candidate's inner aspirations are, what kind of Man he is, whether or not he is good at his job. Money and the mass media help them create an image which will appeal to the public. And what people end up voting for in elections is not so much the Man himself as the image created for him by the political technologists. It won't be long before we'll all be voting for cardboard cut-out politicians and a papier-mâché president!

As for the shaping of images of whole nation-states and their peoples, these are the masterpieces of an incomparably higher-rank species of political technologists.

Centuries of human history have borne witness to a host of examples of controlling a nation-state through images. The most salient and obvious example for people today of the work of these top-ranked political technologists — or

---

[6]*Division 13* — designating the unit of the KGB responsible for covert operations, including sabotage, assassination and even terrorism.

[7]*way of life, way of thinking* — both these terms in Russian contain the word for 'image' (*obraz*).

'modern priests' — may be the history of our country and its peoples over the past century.

We all know about the downfall of the Soviet Union, one of the mightiest empires in the world. But what preceded the formation of the USSR and what gave rise to its subsequent collapse?

Precedent to the formation of the USSR was the creation of an attractive image of a socialist future and then of a communist state. Landowners and manufacturers were cast in the image of bloodsuckers of the proletariat. The tsar still reigned in Russia, and the monarchy seemed unshakeable. Yet at the same time an image was at work which was busy attracting followers, and these in turn found all sorts of ways to bring down the monarchy and create a new state — in the new image.

The fall of the USSR was also preceded by the creation of an image — an image of the country as a totalitarian state, along with a discussion on the need to replace it with a new one — a happy, free democratic state along Western lines. The government and leaders of the communist state were cast in the role of bloodthirsty thugs trampling on freedoms and on the people themselves. The socialist order was painted as intolerable and leading nowhere. The image of communists created by theatre and cinema directors, actors and artists, on which whole generations of the populace had been raised, was now summarily shunted aside. But what was there to take its place?

The resulting vacuum began to be filled with images of flourishing businessmen, gangsters, prostitutes and Hollywood starlets. Our young people strove to imitate their habits and morals. There is no disputing the fact that material wealth is fast becoming the criterion by which prosperity is measured. Who attains it and how — that doesn't enter into the picture. The need to build a developed democratic state has been proclaimed to all, but not a word has been (or is being) said about the insurmountable problems in other 'democratic' countries — drug addiction, colossal corruption, environmental degradation, mental depression, decline in birth-rate and a whole lot else besides.

Women naturally refuse to have children when they see no future for their offspring.

Never mind that people in democratic countries have no clear picture of their own future — our modern 'priests' find it necessary to present democracy in its present form as the only acceptable order for the structuring of human society. Why? Because the conditions of democracy as we know it make it the easiest system to control. It is all too easy to hide behind freedom of speech, freedom of business, freedom of choice and meanwhile throw the public a black lie. And this is done not by happenstance, but deliberately and with considerable forethought. Whatever image you latch on to, you yourself will become.

These political technologists know what will happen next with the whole population. It's not a difficult task to determine who's behind the disasters happening in Russia. All one has to do is track where the country's precious human and financial resources are being siphoned off to each time.

The huge flood of emigration which fled Russia following the 1917 revolution took with it not only a significant amount of capital along with historical treasures and traditions, but, most importantly, human resources.

After the collapse of the Soviet empire, a combination of reforms and a tempting image of prosperous, civilised countries siphoned off (and continues to siphon off) our financial and intellectual resources.

The saddest part is that the latest image of our state is being summoned in the interests of annihilating the whole country and the peoples living therein. No military intervention is required at all. A more significant force than military weaponry is at work here. An *image* is at work. A combination of factors already perceptible to analysts has been put into operation. Quite a simple combination at that. Let's try to reason it through.

What are we building today? Where are we heading to? The political technologists tell us they are building a democratic state on the Western model. And so, once it is built, we shall all be rich and happy.

"But," millions of our fellow-citizens quite reasonably argue, "if there already exist on the Earth developed states that are both democratic and happy, then wouldn't it be easier simply to go and live there now?" And millions *have* left — and continue to leave — for Germany, Israel and America, putting their intellectual and financial capital at the disposal of these countries. And they become slaves there. The image is working!

But what about those left behind in Russia? What are they to do?

"Build a developed democratic state and become rich," says the image. But what can a traffic cop, say, do to build such a state? Or a sales clerk in a store? Or a civil servant in an administrative office? That's not clear to many people. Neither is it clear how one is supposed to become rich on a salary of three to five thousand roubles a month.[8] But quite a number, after all, have somehow managed to wangle their way through. They drive around in expensive cars, build themselves luxury mansions and holiday at fancy resorts. Somehow they've wangled their way through...

And now the whole country is beginning to follow their example. Sales clerks and customers, traffic cops and office

[8] In 2005 (when this book was written) this represented approximately US$100–175, respectively, at the then current exchange rate — or US$200–350 in buying power.

administrators, army officers and private soldiers, teachers and students. But those who know the science of imagery merely scoff at such efforts.

"Come on," they say, "catch a few scapegoats among the officers' ranks. Then you can create a security service within the security service."

Here we are fighting not against causes, but against effects. The image has already done its work. It is capable of entering unhindered into the minds of politicians and generals, high-ranking government officials and ordinary people. Because it is *image,* it knows neither border guards nor closed office doors. It lures young girls from isolated Russian villages to far-away lands with its promises of a happy life, and then forces them to work as prostitutes in Cyprus, Israel or New York.

For the sake of this promise of a happy life, officials are ready to take bribes and policemen to go into cahoots with criminals. This image has tremendous energy. In the meantime, all our politicians can do is keep mouthing over and over hackneyed phrases like *developed democratic countries, the civilised West,* thereby serving to reinforce the image that is so destructive to our country.

People are aware there's something wrong with the country, and so they understand when you, Vladimir Vladimirovich,[9] attempt to impose order, but how to accomplish this? Just consolidating your hold on power is not enough. In doing this you are strengthening not just your own power, but the power of the images too.

Thousands of government officials now have more power, but being under the influence of the image, they will unwittingly act in the interests of the image, i.e., in the interests of the image's creators. But the creators have already decided that Russia's fate is sealed. Their actions have become

[9]*Vladimir Vladimirovich* — President Putin's first name and patronymic.

unbridled and brazenly bold. Specially trained personnel have been sent to Russia for the purpose of strengthening the creators' power by supporting an image which can only destroy the country. I can officially state that right at this moment specially trained people are operating on Russian territory — people whose job it is to keep track of, and correct where necessary, the ideological component of the state. I have a feeling you, Mr President, are aware of this, too.

Let us give some thought as to why there have been so few positive images over the past few years in our nation's literature, film and TV programmes — images capable of inspiring people, setting a pattern to follow and helping build a marvellous future for their children. We still remember and live by those images, but our children?

We are assured that this is the demand of the majority, that everybody wants to watch only Hollywood starlets, gangster showdowns and sensational reports on bloody happenings. Nonsense! That's not what people want! We are told: if you don't want it, then don't watch — if you don't like it, don't listen. That is called freedom of choice. But that's not quite the way it is. Or, rather, that's not the way it is at all. There *is* no choice here! Not for children, not for adults and certainly not for senior citizens. And unless you happen to be cold-hearted, cynical and soulless, you'll discover the road to the promised prosperity is blocked. And there is no other road. Isn't that the case all around you? Or all around us?

All this depravity is being deliberately foisted upon us. Special covert selection mechanisms were put in place long ago. Any poets, innovative educators, writers and directors who have dared create positive images for Russia are cruelly persecuted. Everything is simply closed to them.

This is partly the work, too, of Western spy agencies that claim to be fighting sectarianism. You can hear such declarations coming from the mouths not just of Russian special-service agents, but from social and political activists as well, including the highest officials of the Russian President's administration — your administration. For example, Mr Surkov,[10] your Deputy Chief of Staff, said during a newspaper interview:

> A secret war is being waged against Russia by circles in America, Europe and the Orient, who still regard our country as a potential enemy. They consider themselves to have rendered a service in fostering the virtually bloodless collapse of the Soviet Union, and now they are attempting to capitalise on their success. Their goal is none other than the destruction of Russia and the filling of its vast spaces with a multitude of petty quasi-states.

Such a statement is entirely plausible, even if just because the forces that overthrew the USSR still exist and, quite naturally, not satisfied with having achieved victory at one stage, they will definitely continue with a stepped-up offensive.

And it is especially important here not just to state facts but to understand the mechanism by which the destructive influence operates.

We already know that the collapse of the USSR was brought about not through armed invasion but as the result of an ideological manipulation of our people. Ideology — that is the principal means of either annihilating or reinforcing any nation-state. But any ideology can be used to influence masses of people if it has a well-built and efficient operating structure. It exists and it is not ours. It is not *our* images that are

---

[10]*Vladislav Yurevich Surkov* (1964–) — the Russian President's Deputy Chief of Staff since 1999. During the previous decade and a half Surkov held executive positions with various Russian financial institutions and media organisations.

acting through it. But where has our own structure disappeared to? *We destroyed it!*

In the USSR, apart from its ideological institutions and broadcast centres, the ideological departments of the Communist Party's Central Committee, the Ministry of Culture and the press, there was a huge network including so-called 'Palaces of Culture' and 'Houses of Culture',[11] along with urban and rural district activity clubs.

Such institutions afforded the opportunity for millions of young Soviet citizens to engage in amateur artistic and performance circles, including the holding of lectures and meetings, as well as the opportunity for the accepted state ideology to get through and be explained to the masses.

At the beginning of *perestroika,* when the ideology changed, this network of institutions was liquidated — their financing was cut off.

It is difficult to imagine that a driver motoring along the highway who suddenly realises he is heading in the wrong direction, instead of turning around and heading the right way, begins to dismantle his car on the spot. But something like that is what has happened in our country. When the decision was taken in society (not without the aid of certain forces, of course) that we were heading in the wrong direction, instead of turning around and using existing institutions, they were simply dismantled. And what was there to take their place?

It was proposed to hand over the basic task of spiritually educating the population, especially the youth, to Russia's Orthodox Church. However, more and more testimonies are indicating that, first and foremost, it is necessary to educate the majority of the clergy itself.

---

[11]*Palaces of Culture, Houses of Culture* (Russian: *Dvortsy kul'tury, Domá kul'tury*) — These functioned along the lines of community centres, including concert halls and recreation centres, to provide ideologically approved entertainment and recreational facilities for the public in Soviet times.

As an institution of spirituality, Russia's Orthodox Church was catastrophic in its failure to justify the hopes placed in it. Why? Simply because, through the help of the State, it only took a few years to open twenty thousand churches, while it requires centuries and a host of strict conditions to educate twenty thousand highly spiritual clerics who are truly capable of comforting and educating other people.

And not the kind of conditions as when the state pours forth grants and favours, which only corrupt and attract opportunists and vagabonds. In that scenario the winners are not those pastors who are rich in spirit but those who are more devious and position themselves closer to the trough. It is not the congregation led by a spiritually minded prior that comes out on top, but the one that manages to obtain financing.

After all, the process of attracting parishioners and raising their level of spirituality is a lengthy one — it can drag on for years. So the village priest is obliged to mend his own frock, unable to afford a new one, while his urban counterpart drives around in an expensive foreign car.

This acquisitiveness and covetousness already plaguing the clerics of Russia's Orthodox Church was brought up during a speech at the annual meeting of the Moscow Diocese in the Cathedral Church of Christ the Saviour[12] on 15 December 2004 by Alexei II,[13] the Holy Patriarch of Moscow and all the Russias, when he said:

[12] *Cathedral Church of Christ the Saviour* (Russian: *Kafedral'nyj sobornyj khram Khrista Spasitelia*) — the seat of the Moscow Patriarchate of the Russian Orthodox Church. The original church, built in the early part of the nineteenth century to commemorate deliverance from Napoleon's armies during the War of 1812, was blown up on Stalin's orders in 1931. After World War II the site was used to construct the world's largest swimming pool. The cathedral was reconstructed on the site in the mid-1990s, following the collapse of the communist régime.

Today we are obliged to confront a series of negative phenomena — including the general static state of the church's activity, the absence of dynamics in congregational life, the low attendance by worshippers at temple services and the lack of interest in religion on the part of the rising generation.

The growing commercialisation of many aspects of congregational life is an alarming indicator of the dying out of the Orthodox consciousness, spiritual blindness and the disparagement of ecclesiasticism. Material self-interest all too often comes to the fore, overshadowing and stamping out everything living and spiritual. All too often temples deal in 'church services' as though they were commercial firms.

Nothing pushes people away from the faith as much as the selfishness of priests and others who serve in the temples. It is with good reason that covetousness is termed a hateful, murderous passion and the only treason in respect to God — in other words, a hellish sin.

The Patriarch outlawed taking payment for performing church sacraments — the rituals of communion, marriage, last rites and burial services — as well as commercialising the 'services' of the Church. But will clerics heed the ban imposed by the supreme church hierarchy, if they already transgress a higher law — the commandments of God?

---

[13] *Alexei II* (also spelt in English: Alexius II) — the spiritual head of the Russian Orthodox Church. Born Alexei Mikhailovich Ridiger in 1929 in Estonia, in 1990 Alexei II was chosen *Patriarch of Moscow and of All the Russias* (*Patriarkh Moskovsky i vseya Rusi*).

Russia's Orthodox Church — but is it Russia's?

Apart from everything else, Western spy agencies have exerted what may be the strongest and most destructive influence on Russia's Orthodox Church (ROC).[14] And this could have been foreseen, of course, if someone had only been assigned to foresee it. We know that major shifts in our country are always preceded by an ideological makeover. Could the departments of Western spy agencies responsible for the transformations in Russia required by their masters leave untouched such an important institution as ROC? Of course not! Otherwise their work would not be professional. Besides, the conditions in Russia at the time offered more than fertile ground for ideological diversion. Occupied with their own reorganisation, *our* spy agencies, to put it mildly, were busy with their internal 'settling of accounts', which I believe is still going on.

It is impossible to know about every single operation perpetrated by a Western spy agency through ROC structures. But one in particular has struck a chord in society as a whole. Millions of Russia's citizens, including the Church's own clerics, have felt and continue to feel its destructive consequences. I'm talking here about the agency formed under the ægis of ROC which labels as 'sects' a wide range of secular and religious organisations, thus provoking negative reactions to ROC on their part.

---

[14]*Russia's Orthodox Church* (Russian: *Rossiiskaya Pravoslavnaya Tserkov*) — traditionally known as the Russian (*Russkaya*) Orthodox Church. Note that the author deliberately uses the word *Rossiiskaya* in this phrase, emphasising its association with Russia (*Rossiya*) or the Russian Federation (*Rossiiskaya Federatsiya*) as a political entity, rather than *Russkaya*, which is used more in reference to the Russian people, language and culture. See also Book 7, especially footnote 11 in Chapter 15: "Opposition", as well as footnote 3 in Chapter 20: "Pagans".

These 'anti-sectarians' have been acting in the name of the Church and even, as they claim, with the blessing of Patriarch Alexei II. In response to their actions people who formerly maintained a tolerant attitude toward the Church or even attended services as baptised members, have now simply torn off the crosses they used to wear around their necks.

One more ploy of the 'anti-sectarians': in working to expose their straw-man 'sects', they virtually criticised and brought shame upon Russia's Orthodox Church itself, dealing it a serious blow. After that, they decided to take control of the higher organs of state power in the Russian Federation.

Having accepted the idea of a marvellous future for Russia (as shown in these books) with their heart and soul, people in various parts of Russia have turned (and continue to turn) to local administrations, asking them to grant them plots of land for the setting up of family domains. And, what is truly amazing, people for the first time are not asking for favours, or salary or pension supplements, but simply a small piece of their country's natural landscape where they can create their own living (and not just survival) conditions.

It would seem that this impulse which has arisen among the public is something that ought to be welcomed with open arms. And this impulse is no fly-by-night whim, but a lasting, well-thought-through desire, as the past four years will attest. This idea has encompassed various segments of the population: school pupils, scholars and entrepreneurs, teachers, doctors and pensioners, soldiers and politicians, artists, poets and writers — including academicians,[15] governors and the wives of presidents of former Soviet republics.

These people can help not only in solving many of the socio-economic problems our country is facing, but also in

[15] *academicians* — members of the Russian Academy of Sciences (a very high rank indeed).

making drastic improvements in our country's demographic situation, unemployment rate and national health, as well as in securing safe food supplies. But the main thing is to harness the mighty force of the people themselves, who, in creating their own Space, will strengthen their beloved country and nation-state which has afforded them the opportunity to do so.

Evidently, however, there is someone who is greatly displeased by these positive aspirations which have emerged in the Russian people.

Occupiers in action

Certain government agencies at the regional (and sometimes even local) level have been advised to treat the readers of my books as sectarians and terrorists, and, consequently, to counteract any initiative they may undertake, especially those wishing to set up their own family domains in rural areas. The mass media were ordered, under threat of sacking journalists, not to report on these initiatives. Or if there were any reference, it had to describe them as part of the 'loony fringe', calling everybody to go to the forest, back into the past etc. People working in the cultural sector were called upon to take countermeasures against anything connected with the books or the ideas set forth therein.

Communications from readers clearly point to the activities of some sort of organisation operating on our national territory through agents in state and ecclesiastical structures and carrying out destructive policies. And don't just take *my* word for it. This is confirmed by professional researchers who have familiarised themselves with a significant body of collected materials.

A special term has even surfaced: 'the Anastasia cult'. And to whom or to what does this term specifically refer? To me as a writer? To my *Anastasia* book? To the book's heroine, whose name is Anastasia? To the millions of readers of these books? Or to their efforts to implement Anastasia's idea about a marvellous and prosperous Russia? As it turns out, all of the above.

It is a sad sight indeed to see both foreign and home-grown clerics — who are definitely not of any Christian faith — occupying the Orthodox Church and exerting their influence on state officials. Christianity for them is only a convenient cover. Their actions show clearly that they are far removed from any Christian morality. Their methods are 'old hat' — the same methods of falsehood and violence that were used to destroy the culture of Ancient Rus' in favour of a new ideology foreign to the people. I have written about this in my books.[16]

Right off they began accusing me of paganism. But what kind of an 'accusation' is that? It's tantamount to accusing me of the desire to know the history of my country and the culture of my forebears.

There is, however, some very happy, encouraging news. Life has begun more and more often to come out with situations where their unseemly actions are exposed as if by an invisible ray of light. It puts them, one might say, in a rather funny predicament. Judge for yourselves.

---

[16]See, for example, Book 7, Chapter 20: "Pagans", especially footnotes 3 & 4.

CHAPTER TEN

The Book of Kin and *A Family Chronicle*

In 2002 Dilya Publishers[1] issued the next book in the Ringing Cedars Series entitled *Rodovaya kniga* (The Book of Kin), in which it advised its readers:

> Our publishing house has taken the idea of a 'Book of Kin' to heart. As we were getting this book ready for press, we decided to set at once about publishing a blank 'Book of Kin' for you to fill in and thereby keep a record of your own family chronicle.

Not long after Dilya published this *Family Chronicle,* in 2003 the Russky Dom[2] publishing house put out a book under the title *Semeinaya letopis* (A family chronicle). One of its compilers was Archimandrite Tikhon Shevkunov.[3]

At the front of the book were featured guest forewords by Russian President Vladimir Putin and Alexei II,[4] Patriarch of Moscow and of All the Russias.

---

[1]*Dilya Publishers* — the current publishers of the Russian edition of the Ringing Cedars Series, located in St Petersburg and Moscow. The quotation cited did not appear in the English edition of *The Book of Kin*.

[2]*Russky Dom* (lit. 'Russian House') — the name of (a) a publishing-house in Moscow related to the Russian Orthodox Church and (b) a monthly magazine it publishes. Archimandrite Tikhon sits on the magazine's editorial board.

[3]*Archimandrite Tikhon Shevkunov* — Archimandrite (Father Superior) of the Sretensky Monastery in Moscow, sometimes described as a spiritual advisor to President Putin.

A family chronicle is not just a simple story about a few human destinies, or even about a whole family. It tells the story of a whole nation. The destiny of Russia is the history of families over successive generations.

Such knowledge is indispensable for each citizen of Russia to become aware of his roots and his role in the history of our great Motherland.

— Vladimir Vladimirovich Putin, President of Russia

The atmosphere of the family and home, relations with one's relations, memories of one's forebears and the raising of one's descendants — all this has tremendous implications for the moral strengthening of the individual and, consequently, of the nation. It is no coincidence that it is said among many different peoples that love for one's Motherland begins at home.

— Alexei II, Patriarch of Moscow and of All the Russias

The first one to put forward this idea was Anastasia:[5]

Just a few days will go by, and millions of fathers and mothers in many a land will be writing their Book of Kin, filling in its pages with their own hand. There will be a vast multitude of them — these Books of Kin. And all of them will contain the truths which begin in the heart, for their children. There will be no room in these books for artifice or guise. Before them all the lies of history will fall.

— Anastasia

We shan't go into details as to how Russky Dom followed the example of Dilya or who was responsible. The important

---

[4]*Alexei II* — see footnote 13 in Chapter 9: "A fine state of affairs!" above.

[5]Quoted from Book 6, Chapter 10: "The Book of Kin".

thing is the implementation of the idea itself. Now we can see that this idea has the support of the President, the Patriarch and the Chairman of the State Duma,[6] who presented copies of *A Family Chronicle* to schoolchildren on Knowledge Day.[7]

Now what are the poor slanderers to do? Include the President, the Patriarch and the Chairman of the State Duma in their list of sectarians? Along with the former President of Ukraine, who signed a decree regarding family farms, granting Ukrainians not one, but two hectares of land each?

And we must not forget Governor Ayatskov,[8] who during an interview on NTV[9] said of Anastasia's followers: "The future of the country lies with them." He has also encouraged his civil service staff to acquire land and set up their own family domains.

Nor Governor Tuleev[10] of the Kemerovo Region, who has granted land for a settlement. Nor the Supreme Mufti of Russia, Talgat Tajuddin,[11] who responded to a question by a

---

[6] *State Duma* (pron. *DOO-ma*) — the lower chamber of the Russian national parliament, corresponding to the House of Commons in the United Kingdom and Canada or the House of Representatives in America, Australia, and New Zealand.

[7] *Knowledge Day* (Russian: *Den' znaniy*) — 1 September, the traditional start of the Russian school year.

[8] *Dmitry Fedorovich Ayatskov* (1950–) — Governor of the Saratov Region on the middle reaches of the Volga River.

[9] *NTV* — abbreviation for *Nezavisimoe televidenie* (lit. 'Independent Television'), a national private TV network created in 1993, which on its Internet site boasts more than 120 million viewers.

[10] *Aman-Gel'dy Moldagazyevich Tuleev* (1944–) — Governor of the Kemerovo Region in Siberia, on the Tom' River (a tributary of the Ob) just to the east of Novosibirsk.

[11] *Talgat Safich Tajuddin* (1948–) — Supreme Mufti (spiritual leader) of Russia's Muslims, formally known as the Chairman of the Central Spiritual Directorate of Muslims of Russia and the European Nations of the Commonwealth of Independent States.

Sotvorenie Studios correspondent — as to what he thought
of the Ringing Cedars Series — as follows:

> I love these books. I read them and get a great deal out
> of them. I feel that reading these books helps strength-
> en Man's faith in God. After all, we need to nourish our
> faith in God day by day. But for that it is not only our eyes
> that must be open — more importantly, our heart must be
> open. Besides, our heart has been given to us for to love,
> and Vladimir Nikolaevich Megré's books help us love God.
> He conveys this truth to people through the words of
> Anastasia.
>
> Perhaps theologians may have some reservations.
> Perhaps someone will call it just a hypothesis, but faith in
> God — and especially love for God — is something that
> starts growing bit by bit, and afterward becomes immeas-
> urable. And long before we get to the next world, right
> here in this world Man can become happy. And the Ringing
> Cedars Series helps us do this.

On the eve of these events, evidently under pressure of the
machinations and fear-mongering of these same 'anti-sectarians', one Orthodox archbishop (I shall not give his name, so
as not to immortalise him) signed a letter threatening to ex-
communicate from the Church anyone who reads or distrib-
utes the Ringing Cedars books.

This would mean that the archbishop would 'excommu-
nicate' the Patriarch himself, who has supported the idea in
creating *A Family Chronicle,* containing his and the President's
signed forewords. Even if the Patriarch has never even held
any of my books in his hands, that's not the point — it's not
the paper with the printed text of the books, after all, that's
important, but the ideas set forth in them. Now that one of
the ideas has been approved, I am convinced that it won't be

long before others will be granted official State support. But in the meantime...

So perhaps it is time we drew the attention of our law-enforcement agencies to just who these so-called 'anti-sectarians' really are. By what methods or machinations do they operate, hiding so conveniently beneath the vaulted ceilings of Russia's Orthodox Church? Evidently, they're not there for prayers! The fomenting of interreligious discord, the discrediting of government agencies — that's what they're really up to.

And it would be foolish to even suppose that some group of 'anti-sectarians' is that strongly concerned about my personal spiritual development. Their actions, rather, are testimony to their carrying out orders to stop any positive transformations from taking place in Russia. An illustration of their ideologically based diversionary tactics may be seen in the following example as well.

The Jewish question

Recently, for the umpteenth time already over the past millennium, passions have been inflamed over the 'Jewish question'.

There has been more and more talk about the spread in both Europe and Russia of extremist views, including anti-Semitism. The European Jewish Congress has linked this situation with the growth of Muslim populations in European countries, which are, they say, aggressively anti-Jewish. But there are many concrete historical examples testifying to the fact that aggression can be deliberately provoked. And this is now actively being pursued by certain circles. The provokers may even come from the ranks of the Jews themselves.

One has the impression that some kind of order has been received regarding the organisation of pogroms. Jewish pogroms are very profitable to someone, and I'm talking about financial profit. Extremist organisations do not derive any financial benefit from pogroms — rather, they suffer losses. But these pogroms offer a palpable benefit to countries where Jewish members of the financial oligarchy flee to legalise their multibillion-dollar incomes and obtain international immunity from prosecution.

And for the sake of such financial benefit they are ready to subject to abuse ordinary and utterly harmless Jews living on Russian territory. This has happened over and over again in the annals of the long-suffering Jewish people.

What's the point of a pogrom? The logic is simple. Public opinion is turning against the oligarchs, the financial magnates, as never before. According to government statistics, approximately 70% of Russia's population believe that they should be immediately censured and dispossessed. Acting on the basis of law, the President, the Government and the Russian Prosecutor's Office are attempting to investigate the activity of a number of oligarchs. They have declared war on corruption and it appears as though over the next four years the oligarchs may indeed be obliged to forfeit their financial holdings. Given the situation, they are naturally trying to get out of the country.

But then there is the problem of how to legalise their transfer of capital to the West. The surest way is to provoke a kind of pogrom that will shock the world community. It's easy to see what happens next. The financial magnates simply turn up in one of the Western countries while these pogroms are going on and declare themselves political refugees. Naturally this provides them with not only political asylum but also a legalisation of their financial holdings, even while they may still maintain at least partial control over resources and factories back home through dummy CEOs or trusted associates.

And herein lies an important message for all Russian citizens, especially those organisations which call themselves patriotic. Don't ever give in to provocation or stoop to the level of organising pogroms against synagogues. You will only be acting out somebody else's script.

It would be wrong to accuse all Jews of machinations and unseemly acts. Just like Russians, Belarusians and Ukrainians, Jews come in all stripes and colours. I offer the following as proof. I was once the featured speaker at a readers' conference in Kazan,[12] where the audience was comprised of different nationalities, including many Muslims. During my remarks I read a chapter from a book by the Jewish writer and poet Efim Kushner[13] entitled *Beskrovnaya revoliutsiya* (A bloodless revolution). Before reading from it, I said that this was a Jewish writer living in Israel but writing about Russia, about her future. When I had finished reading the chapter, the hall broke into thunderous applause.

Muslims, too, applauded this Jewish writer and poet. Why? How did it happen that supposedly aggressive Muslims offered their sincere applause to a Jewish writer?

[12]*Kazan* — capital of the Republic of Tatarstan (within the Russian Federation), about 1,000 km east of Moscow. The Republic has a predominantly Muslim population.

[13]*Efim Kushner* (1940–) — Jewish poet and writer, who emigrated to Israel in 1990. The book mentioned was published in 2003 (it appeared in a Bulgarian translation in 2006) and includes favourable comments on the ideas set forth in the Ringing Cedars Series. Another reference to Kushner may be found in footnote 14 in Book 4, Translator's and Editor's Afterword: "Hope for the world".

It happened because in his book he speaks about the marvellous future of Russia, linking it to the ideas outlined in the Ringing Cedars Series. He calls upon the Russian government to adopt a programme based on these ideas.

I can tell you right off that he is not the only Jew who accepts and supports Anastasia's concept set forth in the books. In Israel there is a whole club of readers who have been drawn to the books about this Siberian recluse. Israelis are composing songs in both Russian and Hebrew about the characters in the series. I have the distinct impression that in the final analysis, it will be the Jews who take the lead in putting the ideas into practice, and will draw peoples of many lands along in their wake.

I can at least tell you that I have been informed that right there in Israel significant funds have been set aside for the construction of environmentally clean settlements.

"Oh, those connivers!" people will say later on. "See, they're stealing the Russian idea out from under us!"

Pardon me, but they are not stealing anything from us. In fact, they are saving this idea! Will you kindly tell me who is preventing the Russian authorities from implementing the ideas in the books? After all, for the past five years, practically, it is these same authorities that have been targeted with a large number of individual and collective letters by Russians living in the Commonwealth of Independent States and elsewhere in the world.

It is truly a comical situation that has developed. A host of researchers keep talking about the birth of a 'national idea' among the Russian people. But the way things are turning out here, it looks as though it will have its first implementation in Israel! Who's to blame?

Overall, every discussion on the Jewish question so far, at least those in the publications I have access to, seems pretty primitive. Almost all of them boil down to a routine statement

of the facts: "Jews have taken over the press in various countries." "Pretty much all the TV networks are in Jewish hands."
"Most cash flow is controlled by Jews."

All this is no doubt true, including here in Russia today.
But this is simply a statement of fact and nothing more. It
is far more important to explain *why* situations like this have
developed in various countries, with an enviable consistency,
over a period of centuries.

I can tell you the following right off. It is simply that the
Jews are obliged to do this, and we are obliged to fall into line
with them, including on the legislative level.

Judge for yourselves: the State Duma of the Russian
Federation adopted a law recognising four 'basic' religions,
two of which are Christianity and Judaism.

According to Christianity, the Christian is the 'slave'[14] of
God. Wealth is not welcomed. In St Petersburg, where I am
writing these lines, I can see from my hotel window the huge
Orthodox Cathedral of the Blessed Virgin of Vladimir, on the
façade of which is written in large, gold lettering: *Hear, Our
Lady, the prayer of thy slave.*[15]

According to Judaism, the Jew is the chosen one of God; to
him belong wealth and lands, and usury[16] is welcomed.

[14]Note that Russia's Orthodox Church traditionally refers to every human
individual as 'slave of God' (*rab Bozhii*). It is reflected even in the contemporary Russian word for 'worker' (*rabochii*), which literally means 'Father's
slave'. The term is generally translated 'servant' in the Authorised Version
of the English Bible.

[15]Compare the wording of Daniel 9: 17: "O our God, hear the prayer of thy
servant..." Note, too, that in this citation the Russian term corresponding
to *Our Lady* is *vladychitsa,* which has the connotation of 'empress' or 'high
ruler'. The Russian term corresponding to *the Blessed Virgin of Vladimir* is
Vladimirskoi Bozhei Materi, lit. 'the Vladimir Mother of God'.

[16]See, for example, Deut. 23: 20: "Unto a stranger thou mayest lend upon
usury" (*Authorised King James Version*), rendered in the *New English Bible* as:
"You may charge interest on a loan to a foreigner".

Everybody knows what a huge influence religions exercise on Man's mentality, character development and way of life.

So let us be consistent in the logic of our actions. The highest legislative organ of our land has accepted these two concepts, at the same time designating who is to be slave and who is to be ruler.

And, being the law-abiding citizens that we are, let us not keep deceiving each other, but let us accept as a given, according to the law adopted by our government, that the Jews have authority over us.

Now there are some that will not be satisfied with such a position. Some will even consider such a statement absurd. But let us not close our eyes to the actualities of life. Let us see clearly the causes of what is going on, or we shall keep on tasting the consequences with an unyielding regularity.

If someone is unhappy over the current situation, then by all means let us work together to find an alternative.

The solution might be an idea acceptable with equal enthusiasm to Muslims, Christians, Jews and members of other faiths.

Such an idea exists. Not only will it fix the situation, but it holds the future in its hands. There are specific facts and life situations that attest to this.

Let's create

In an address to the Federal Assembly,[17] the President of the Russian Federation set a goal of doubling the country's Gross

Domestic Product (GDP) within ten years. Well, a goal is a goal. And measures must be taken to reach it. The first step is to inspire the people with a vision. It is the people, after all, who must work to double GDP indicators. And what has been happening since this goal was set by the highest official in the current government?

Incredible events began to take place.

Instead of at least making an attempt at realising the goal, some highly placed officials began talking about how unfeasible its implementation was, while others insisted it still must be attained. And that's it! Nothing more. These discussions have wasted precious time: the year 2004 ended miserably, with a GDP growth of a mere 6.4%.

Right from the start this fascinating subtext as to whether the goal was feasible or not ran throughout the whole treatment of the subject by the press. But, again, with not even a single attempt at implementation.

This situation points to the fact that the Russian authorities are heading for a state of utter helplessness. And it makes no difference here whether the officials in question are elected or unelected, they will find any excuse they can not to carry out the directive.

Imagine how it would be if a commander-in-chief gave the order to *prepare to attack,* and his generals and colonels, instead of working out the plan of attack, began to discuss whether an attack was feasible or not. In that case defeat would be an inevitability. Which is exactly what has happened.

But could it be possible that the goal set by the President was really preposterous? We can't judge until we try to figure

---

[17]*Federal Assembly* (Russian: *Federal'noe sobranie*) — the name given to the bicameral Russian Parliament as a whole, which comprises the State Duma (or lower chamber) and the Federation Council (upper chamber), as established by the 1993 Constitution of the Russian Federation.

it out for ourselves. However, I'll jump ahead of myself and say: *it is feasible!*

I can just see my readers' dumbfounded reaction: what's all this about Russia's Orthodox Church, 'anti-sectarians', Western intelligence services and the goal set by the President for doubling Russia's GDP? Be patient. There is a very close mutual connection here.

Think who would benefit by a doubling of Russia's GDP. Russia herself, of course. Who would lose by it? Naturally, the West, which looks upon Russia merely as an overflow market for its substandard merchandise.

And Western intelligence services, it seems, have once again had the upper hand (as usual), putting down the Russian President and his officials, ridiculing them even as the afore-mentioned goal was being set. But let's go step by step.

In order to double the overall GDP, it is necessary to first identify those economic sectors where an increase in output is essential, as well as those where such an increase would be undesirable — the production of tobacco, wine and spirits, for example (Russia's already drowning in her own booze and choking on her own tobacco smoke). You wouldn't want to double the output of armaments, or build new casinos, or double the outflow of raw materials from the country.

Which means that the remaining sectors of the economy are faced with the task of not just doubling but tripling or even quadrupling their output. These sectors have not yet been identified and, consequently, no specific goal has ever been suggested to them.

Well, some may object, if we're not sure we can double our GDP or not, how can we even think in terms of quadrupling? An impossible task!

But I say *it is possible!* It is possible, and not only that, but it requires no additional capital investment.

Take agriculture, for example, where production has been cutting back year after year, to the point where it has already begun to threaten national security. It is the talk of politicians, Duma deputies and a number of government officials.

But they're not talking in the wind. In the case of some food categories, imports already account for up to 40% of the market. This is already a threat to our national security. And what awaits us after that? I'll tell you.

By 2005 our country's rural population is expected to shrink by 25%, which will exacerbate the problem even further. More specifically, it will make the country completely dependent on external sources — and then the government will be forced to pay for food not just with natural resources, but through sales of missiles, just to avoid being utterly torn to pieces by the population at large.

This means a sea-change is required in the whole agriculture industry: it must double or even triple its production. However, this will never happen using traditional methods, where all proposals simply come down to nothing more than a requirement for additional subsidies. And it is not clear just who these subsidies are to be directed to, given that the able-bodied rural population keeps significantly decreasing in numbers. And if that be the case, not even the most state-of-the-art equipment or super-technology is going to help. There will simply be nobody left to work with it.

Which means that our goal is first and foremost to have able-bodied people showing up in the countryside. Millions of them. Tens of millions. Not only that, but they must be people with a desire to reach out and touch the ground with love. If *they* don't show up, there's no point in talking about anything else.

To hear some officials tell it, however, getting people to show up like that would be nothing short of a miracle. It is not something they believe in. They haven't believed in it even when it's happened.

Yes, ladies and gentlemen, the miracle *has* happened!

All thanks to one individual — the Siberian recluse named Anastasia.

Maybe her words seem incredible and fantasaical to some, but they are right on. They have given birth to an enduring impulsion in people's hearts and souls.

Tens of thousands of people in various parts of the country have been wanting to chart their life-course in a rural setting — to set up their domains there and move in. The numbers of applicants are rising with each passing year.

They are setting up their own regional action groups and demanding: *GIVE US LAND! We are ready to take care of it.*

These people have united in a non-governmental organisation, which was founded at a conference in the city of Vladimir on 5 June 2004 — an event which showed, for the first time in post-Soviet Russia, the rise of a popular force unparalleled in modern times. The hall was filled to capacity, as many came who were not registered delegates but simply wanted to listen and tune in to what was happening.

By a vote taken at the conference, a people's movement was set up under the name *Ringing Cedars of Russia,* with the basic aim of supporting the idea of kin's domains. It was truly a people's movement, opposed to neither the government nor any political party. Rather, it aimed to reach out to all with the simple message: *Let's create.*

Thus a people's movement was born with a clear and distinct programme, easily comprehensible to and solidly supported by the public.

What benefit would accrue to the State of Russia by carrying out just one platform of this programme? Outwardly, it is a very simple platform, focusing on a single hectare of land, but envisaging the following wide-ranging results:

- a significant improvement in the environmental situation;

- restoration of soil fertility;
- a solution to the question of providing high-quality produce for the country's population;
- a significant (twofold or threefold) increase in wages across all sectors of the economy without risk of inflation;
- an immediate improvement in the demographic situation and in the general health of the population, including its rejuvenation;
- a solution to the question of the nation's defence preparedness;
- the termination of capital outflow along with, by contrast, a capital inflow into Russia; the return of her intellectual resources;
- a significant reduction in (over the next few years) and eventual extirpation of: bribery, corruption, gangsterism and terrorism;
- a coming together of neighbouring countries[18] along with those of the former Warsaw Pact (Poland, the Czech Republic, Slovakia, Hungary, Bulgaria and the three Baltic states) into a single powerful union;
- cessation of the arms race and close co-operation among Russia, the USA and Eastern Moslem states.

These points have been worked out not just by me, but also by a number of students in their graduating essays — e.g., the essay by the budding jurist Tatiana Borodina.[19] They are also talked about in scholarly publications (e.g., by Professor Viktor

---

[18] *neighbouring countries* — primarily those of the Commonwealth of Independent States, made up of most of the republics of the former Soviet Union (Ukraine, Belarus, Georgia, Kazakhstan etc.).

[19] Ms Borodina's graduating essay is entitled: "The legal status of Kin's Domains in Ukraine: developmental perspectives", and has been made available on a number of Russian websites.

Yakovlevich Medikov,[20] a three-term deputy of the legislative assembly who holds a doctorate in economics). There are a number of privately published brochures on the topic, written by professional researchers as well as ordinary people.

I shall attempt to jot down a few words of explanation in justification of some of these points.

So, let us suppose that our country has decided to implement the programme proposed by Anastasia:

> *Every willing family is offered free of charge one hectare of land for lifetime use with the right of inheritance for the purposes of establishing on it their own kin's domain. The produce grown on the domain, as well as the domain itself, is not subject to any form of taxation.*

The adoption of this programme will lead to the following results:

• *A significant improvement in the environmental situation.* Practice has shown that people who have received land for a kin's domain first of all set about planting wild-growing trees, at an average of up to 200 trees per family, along with an average of 2,000 shrubs, hedges and berry bushes and 50 fruit-bearing trees.

Even using the most conservative estimates, researchers predict that the adoption of such a programme on a national level, if correctly implemented, will lead, right in its earliest stages, to about ten million Russian families setting up their own kin's domains.

This means that even in the first year or two following the adoption of the programme, and without any additional subsidies, two billion wild-growing trees will have been planted, 20 billion shrubs and approximately 500 million fruit-bearing trees. And that is just the beginning.

• *Restoration of soil fertility.* As can be seen from practice, the first thing people do when they are granted land, not on a short-term lease but for their lifetime use, is to put their efforts into soil restoration. Not only that, but they are doing this not just by the application of organic fertilisers, but also by a more natural method, namely, the sowing of soil-building crops during the early years.

• *A solution to the question of providing high-quality produce for the country's population.* You may remember the 'struggle for the harvest'[21] back in Soviet times — how schoolchildren, students and industrial employees were transported out to collective and state-owned farms[22] to help bring in the harvest.

---

[21] *struggle for the harvest* (Russ. *bor'ba za urozhai*) — a term used in Soviet propaganda in reference to harvest time. Since collective farms were inherently inefficient, authorities were compelled to mount a campaign each year, urging vast numbers of people — from schoolchildren and students to industrial workers and soldiers — to help with the harvesting and 'save the crops' before they rotted in the field. People were generally expected to carry out this work either with payment in kind or without any remuneration at all.

[22] *collective and state-owned farms* — two systems of agricultural management during the Soviet era. On a collective farm (*kolkhoz,* pron. *kall-HOSS*), it was claimed that workers as a collective owned their farm, sold their produce to the State and shared in the profits from the sale, while on a state-owned farm (*sovkhoz,* pron. *sahf-HOSS*), farm workers were paid a salary, just as in a factory. In reality, however, in both cases the quantities and prices were dictated by the state.

I myself took part in these large-scale operations, weeding fields and gathering onions at a suburban state-owned farm.

However, there was still no abundance of high-quality produce in the country. Today's older generations, of course, remember how the potatoes sold in stores would be half-rotted, not to mention the most undesirable-looking vegetables.

Then came the dacha movement.[23] They began to allot people 600 square metres of land. And a miracle happened. Everyone is aware of the statistics. Ordinary people — all by themselves, without any support from government ministries or agencies — have provided 80% of the vegetables produced in Russia. (Unfortunately, all sorts of complications are being introduced these days, including higher travel fares, taxes on land plots, increased electricity rates.) And all this on just 600 square metres, where it is impossible to create any kind of economically viable enterprise or to plant tall trees which enrich the soil, or to put in water ponds and so forth. And all this carried out by people without sufficient knowledge or experience, working just on weekends and holidays.

A hectare of land will allow the setting up of a more economically viable enterprise. With the right kind of organisation, there will be a thirtyfold decrease in the workload per square metre. Not all at once, mind you, but I do emphasise:

---

[23]The term *dacha* (originally from the verb *davat'* = to give/grant), dates back to at least the eleventh century. It has had a variety of meanings, including country residences of the Russian cultural and political élite. From the 1940s on, with the emergence and rapid growth of food gardening by the urban population, the term has been used more and more to denote a country garden plot belonging to a city-dweller, usually together with a small cottage. The *dacha movement* referred to here arose during the Second World War, when the Soviet government began to allot small plots of land for food production to combat war-time food shortages, and has since grown to include approximately 20 million families. For further information, please see Book 1 (especially the Translator's Preface) and Book 2 (notably Chapter 9: "Dachnik Day and an All-Earth holiday!").

it has to be set up properly. That given, both existing practice and theoretical calculations confirm that implementing the proposed programme will fully guarantee the country a sufficient food supply for all its citizens bar none.

Now a word about *quality*. It goes without saying that someone growing agricultural produce to be used by his own family will not add any poisonous chemicals or chemical fertilisers to the soil. He will not grow any mutant produce. All this crap is being imported into our country and bought up by the public for no other reason than insufficient production here at home. Once a sufficient quantity level is reached, *quality* becomes the number one concern. I hope I've made myself clear?

• *A significant (twofold or threefold) increase in wages across all sectors of the economy without risk of inflation and a reduction of prices within the country on all forms of merchandise, leading to a reduction in social tension.* Someone may wonder what possible link there could be between the implementation of the 'Kin's domains' programme and a wage increase — let's say, for a salesman, a trolleybus driver, a nurse or a teacher. But there is! And a direct causal link at that.

Think about it. Most enterprises today are in private hands. People we call oligarchs enjoy fabulous profits — but at whose expense? Basically, at the expense of minimum wage-earners. And what's the point of increasing their wages, let's say, from five thousand to twenty thousand roubles a month,[24] when there are still people queuing up just to get a job? There's simply nowhere for them to go.

---

[24] At the time this book was written (2005), the average wage in Russia was 8,500 roubles per month — approximately equivalent to US$300 at the official exchange rate (or to US$600 in buying power). Wages vary greatly from one region to another, and full income amounts are often unreported (meaning the actual average is higher than that calculated by government agencies).

It's an entirely different situation with a family whose work on their own domain earns them an average of ten thousand roubles a month (which has been proved entirely feasible in practice) with a minimal cost of living. No utility bills or daily commuting expenses, or the cost of buying meals at city cafés. To attract domain dwellers to work in a factory or other private enterprise, one would have to offer them a salary at least one-and-a-half or two times the income they would earn from working on the domain, and cover travel and meal expenses besides.

Today an oligarch who has privatised a factory or oil-drilling company can afford to live in a castle in London (that really happens) and earn up to a million dollars a month, while the workers slaving away to provide that income for him receive less than a tenth of one percent of what he makes.

This scenario can be played out *ad infinitum*. Inevitably it leads to revolution, stripping the property-owner of his enterprises and the overthrow of the government permitting such inequities. The only way to prevent such a result from occurring is to reach an equitable sharing arrangement with the workers. Oligarchs will not come to this point voluntarily but, under pressure of circumstances, will give in.

We mentioned the relationship between a domain dweller and the owner of an industrial enterprise. But those left living in city flats will also see their wages rise, to keep them at their jobs. They too, after all, are given a choice: stay working and living in urban conditions, or start building themselves a whole new way of life in the country.

And one more question on this point: *Why will this not lead to inflation or price rises?*

Inflation is always the outcome of certain concrete procedures, specially engineered. Price rises are simply a by-product. The cause is always Man's estrangement from a natural way of life. It is an easy matter to increase prices on fuel and foodstuffs when people don't have any of either to call their own, meaning that they are completely dependent on external suppliers. But try raising apple prices for someone who has his own orchard. Absurd! And what about fuel? But even here there's a limit. Today's fuel prices are so high that it is actually more profitable to till a couple of hectares of land using horses — which, by the way, supply a first-class fertiliser for the soil.

• *An immediate improvement in the demographic situation and in the general health of the population, including its rejuvenation.* It is no secret that the current demographics in our country are catastrophic. And even *this* word isn't strong enough to describe it fully. If a country's peacetime population decreases by almost a million souls annually, that's monstrous! The leaders of such a country, I should think, would want to hide their identity from the public, as well as from their descendants. Discussions on the need to change the current situation amount to nothing more than pathetic babble. They don't change anything. Not even increasing financial support for birthing mothers, as necessary as that may be, will lead to any substantial improvement.

The history of many millennia shows that women cease giving birth when they see no prospective future for their children. It is necessary first to determine clearly and precisely the future development of society as a whole, as well as of each family making up that society.

The Anastasia Foundation in Vladimir[25] conducted a survey of families planning on setting up their own kin's domains. Of the more than two thousand polled, 1,995 responded that

---

[25]The *Anastasia Foundation for Culture and Assistance to Creativity* — a non-profit organisation based in the city of Vladimir. See Book 5, Chapter 15: "Making it come true".

they would be having children. Some wanted three or even more. Those who for health reasons were unable to have children of their own were planning to adopt them from orphanages. How to explain this phenomenon? It is simply that a Man who has built a marvellous living oasis is aware that he is building something lasting, and wants his children to enjoy life, too.

As to rejuvenation and revitalisation of health, let us turn once more to practice. Look at how much livelier and younger your grandfathers and grandmothers behave once they get out to their dachas in the springtime. And it goes without saying that a pregnant woman who eats only environmentally clean produce, drinks clean water and breathes clean air cannot help but bear healthy children — significantly healthier than today's examples.

• *A solution to the question of the nation's defence preparedness. A significant reduction in weapons and, over the next few years, the eventual complete extirpation of bribery, corruption, gangsterism and terrorism.* The military preparedness and morale of our armed forces today, including the nation's law-enforcement officers, has slipped below the zero-mark and is heading deep into the minus side. It is no secret how challenging it is for local conscription offices to call up young recruits to military service. Refusal of military obligations is no longer considered shameful among today's youth — on the contrary, it has become a mark of bravery. Those whose families are slightly better off attempt to buy their way out of serving; those not so well off try to 'cut out' any way they can, even to the point of self-mutilation.[26]

---

[26]By law, military service is compulsory for all male Russian citizens upon reaching the age of 18.

So it turns out that, by hook or by crook, the army drags in conscripts from the poorest segments of the population. Such an army is in no position to defend anyone or anything against a major enemy. Not only that, but it is potentially dangerous to the very country it is supposed to serve.

Let's take a close look at just *whom* the soldiers of the Russian army are called upon to protect. *The Motherland,* comes the standard response. But today the concept of *Motherland* has been seriously eroded, and it is a challenge to grasp hold of just what *is* one's Motherland. It wasn't that long ago that Russian officers and soldiers swore an oath of allegiance to the USSR, which was also considered their Motherland. Then all at once the borders changed and whole parts of the territory they were defending turned out to be 'foreign soil'. The troops deployed in these parts were suddenly treated as invaders. They were left to defend the people on the part of the territory that was still known as Russia. But what kind of people were they really protecting? Oligarchs and bribe-taking government officials? Their own families? But if a soldier or an officer came from a poor family, who was he supposed to protect them from?

For the past ten years now, government propaganda has proclaimed that we are building "a civilised, democratic state on the Western model". But just think: how could today's Russian soldiers do battle against the forces of NATO or the USA if they have already been brainwashed into thinking that their enemy is civilised and developed, which must mean that 'we', by contrast, are '*un*civilised' and '*un*developed'? Quite absurd. Is this some sort of psychobabble, or a deliberately invented tactic? An all-professional army has been touted as a panacea for getting out of this manufactured dead-end situation, but that is even more absurd. A professional army, as is known, is made up of mercenaries who take up arms for money and shoot at whoever they are told is the target. They carry out the orders of whoever pays the most.

History is full of examples of governments afraid to bring their armies of mercenaries home. That's how it was in Ancient Rome, and a similar danger exists in the USA. It is already happening in parts of Russia as well.

A professional army must be kept busy in continual fighting, preferably not on the territory of the nation it is supposed to be serving. When an army returns to its home country, it will inevitably be in demand by forces opposed to the existing authority, or it will disintegrate into a large number of splinter groups, some of which may even be transformed into criminal gangs. For the most part, there is no such thing as *un*employed armed mercenaries. If they are not given work, they will find it on their own, and in their chosen profession. Besides, an army consisting of people serving only for money can be very easily bought off by a higher bidder.

Just imagine a foreign military base located, say, in Georgia, Turkmenistan or Ukraine, whose soldiers are paid three thousand dollars a month, while ours get only five hundred a month. In fact, you don't need to imagine this. There are already concrete examples right here in Russia. Just look at how many highly qualified and professionally trained officers of the former KGB are now working as security guards for commercial organisations, including foreign banks.

So, what's the solution? There is just one — one and only one. We must make sure that our Russian soldiers, officers and generals have something left to protect.

• *Every Russian army or law-enforcement officer, upon receiving the rank of lieutenant, is to be awarded not only a little star on his epaulette, but at the same time the right to receive a hectare of land on which to set up his kin's domain.* The land grants shouldn't be for 'back lot' waste lands, but for élite lands specially allocated by the government for settlement purposes. An officer should be able to choose his own particular hectare within these territories. And, when home on leave, he should be free to plant, either alone or together with his parents, a new garden, or dig a pond, or designate a spot on which to build a house.

And if he is frequently re-posted to various parts of the country or even abroad, during the time he is billeted in officers' quarters, barracks or a field tent, every officer of the Russian Army should be able to rest secure in the knowledge that back there, in a spot of his own choosing, the garden of his little Motherland — his own garden — is flourishing in the springtime. And the girl who has fallen in love with him will know from the little star on his epaulettes that her beloved has a future, has a Motherland, and a family nest for their future children.

And even if, for the time being, she has to share with her beloved in the challenging conditions of an officer's life, all the same, at least once a year they will visit their little Motherland and share their dreams and plans for the future domain. They will decide where the pond is to be dug and where the house is to be built.

And even if they are obliged to spend their month's leave on their own land in a tent, still they will be able to experience an incomparable sense of joy at beholding the marvellous future that lies ahead for the generations of their family to come.

And even if the little trees of their future garden are still young and the green hedge they have planted around their domain is scarcely noticeable, these are still there, and they will grow and flourish, waiting for them, their creators.

• *If an officer's wife becomes pregnant, within three months' time, the State should build on the designated spot a modest home according to the plans selected by the parents-to-be, with all the amenities afforded by modern technology.* And the wife of a Russian officer will be able to spend the remaining months of her pregnancy in her own little house. Perhaps her home will be shared by her parents, or perhaps she will be alone there, keeping in touch with friendly neighbours. But, most importantly, she will be surrounded and filled by the positive emotions she so badly needs. After all, she will be completely surrounded by the space of her little Motherland, belonging jointly to her and her beloved.

And she won't go off to have her baby overseas or even in one of those incubators we are accustomed to calling, for some reason, *maternity homes.* The officer's wife will have her baby in her own domain, as many women are already doing. Possibly it will be under a doctor's supervision, but it will be at home, in familiar, favourable and sympathetic surroundings — not in some maternity chair which has heard the moans and cries of hundreds of birthing mothers.

• *The child of a Russian officer should be born only in his own family domain.* Even if at the moment of birth the young lieutenant is somewhere far away, he will hear — he will most certainly hear — his child's first joyful cry. And he will let no foe encroach upon his grand Motherland. He, this young lieutenant, a Russian officer, will not let a foe get past him, since at the heart of his vast Motherland is his own little Motherland — one he feels is very dear and close to him, one where his beloved walks in a flourishing garden, holding his wee son by the hand as he takes his own first baby steps in life.

Society! Our society! The society comprising our nation is already today capable of seeing to it that a young mother — the wife of a Russian officer — need not worry about how to get food for her baby. She should be provided for. Maybe not in the style the oligarchs' wives are accustomed to, nor has she any use for the shallow fad of owning a supposedly expensive car. She will have far more than that — love and a future. Her main achievement is the restoration of her Motherland. This is her principal work, her principal task in life.

And society should pay her a salary equal to that of her husband. That's not much, of course, in return for her grand co-creation, but such a step will at least be an initial good-will gesture on the part of society and the State.

Such a possibility already exists right now. Only one shouldn't confuse things by bringing in higher-level economic considerations.

Currently the oil pipeline is showering Russia with a rain of American dollars. And why is not a single drop of this rain falling on any Russian officer, his wife or child, or his little Motherland?

Who thought up such arrangements, concealing themselves behind that supposed panacea for all ills — democracy?

Is it 'democratic' when poorly-paid soldiers or officers of the Russian Army are obliged to defend wealthy oligarchs, their fancy detached houses along the Rublevskoe Highway[27] and their numerous counterparts in other regions of the country? That's not democracy, that's *drivelocracy*!

And if such drivel doesn't change, we shan't have any defence or protection at all. There will be no protection for the average citizen, nor even for the president, let alone the petty and major oligarchs.

The extermination of this drivel will spell an end to corruption, drug trafficking, and the notorious bribe-taking from drivers on the part of traffic cops.

---

[27]*Rublevskoe* (pron. *roob-LYOF-ska-ya*) *Highway* (named for the former village of Rublevo) — an area in the western part of Moscow where many of Russia's *nouveaux-riches* have built or bought expensive apartments or (what used to be a rarity in Moscow) detached single-family homes.

Now tell me: why should a copper have to stand in the street and breathe into his lungs all the roadway dust and the exhaust fumes of all the expensive and not-so-expensive cars passing by? As though they were the cat's pyjamas and he were nothing but a nincompoop. He stands there watching out for their safety, for which he is paid a mere pittance. Indeed, if he didn't take bribes from these cars' owners, he would be ridiculed by his relatives who would think it utterly abnormal; his wife would tear into him and his children would turn away from a father who couldn't even afford to buy them a pair of last season's jeans.

And he is not at all terrified of the police's anti-corruption squads. So what if he's sacked from his job? That's no great loss. It's not a job that will guarantee a living for his family in return for honest labour. It simply means he has to look for another. But what kind of job? What kind of job can he find where he can maintain his integrity and still provide for his family?

And so he stands there in the dust and exhaust fumes and takes his bribes. And for this, society hardly condemns him, but pays him. *So what? — we're all becoming like this,* society thinks. Now *that's* terrifying! The fact that we're getting used to it! We cease dreaming about other possible scenarios. We get accustomed to seeing the crowds of prostitutes, homeless children and street thugs. We get accustomed to the stage shows we call *elections.* Or is someone, in fact, accustoming us to these?

After all, up until recently the most terrifying thing for an inhabitant of a Russian village was social disdain on the part of his fellow-villagers, observing: *She's a slut! He hasn't kept his property up!*

And so, it's time to bring back those days. The time will most certainly come when the most pleasant thing for a Russian citizen to hear will be society's approval in the form of: *He's a good man! He has sensitive and properly behaved children!*

He has a splendid domain! Then there won't be any more crime, corruption or drug trafficking. It will surely come, that time.

On a bench in a shady garden sits a greying, elderly man, tenderly stroking the chestnut-coloured hair of his three-year-old granddaughter, her head nuzzled against his chest, while his eleven-year-old grandson takes the general's greatcoat hanging on the back of the bench and tries it on. Two large general's stars adorn the epaulettes of the greatcoat, which once featured two small lieutenant's stars.

But that's not the most important thing, the grey-headed general thinks, looking at his grandchildren. The most important thing is that he created and saved for his grandchildren this garden, this pond and the whole marvellous Space in his kin's domain, his little Motherland in the heart of Russia. He has saved Russia! And She is flourishing! His Motherland! A fresh cool breeze wafts the fragrance of *Her* gardens around the whole world. And interplanetary winds announce the flourishing of the Earth to other worlds. And the stars in the heavens burn with just a touch of envy, and dream of meeting visitors from the Earth, the wise and bright sons and daughters of God.

It will come to pass! But in the meantime... Do you hear, lieutenants, how the heart of the Russian Land is beating, sounding the alarm?! How it is begging for you to take her, little by little, to yourself and plant gardens? She promises to return to each of you your Spaces of Paradise and give you the gift of eternity!

Do you hear? You must hear!

• *The termination of capital outflow and a new inflow of capital into Russia; the return of her intellectual resources.* I can theoretically prove that this will happen with the adoption of Anastasia's programme in full. This has also been shown theoretically by famous scholarly researchers, as well as by students working on their graduating essays.

There are arguments on both sides here. Only practice can offer incontrovertible proof. And that it has done.

People of the Russian diaspora have been flocking from near and far to communities still under construction — communities which as yet do not have a solid legal footing. I know, for example, just in one community near the city of Vladimir, of a teacher from Turkmenistan and a young couple from America. A similar trend can be observed in many other communities now being built on the territory of Russia and Ukraine. People who can't wait for a law on land grants are buying up land, endeavouring to work within existing legislation. They are buying back their Motherland. It is the duty of society and the State to refund their money. Otherwise there will be a curse hanging over the head of anyone who has seen fit to take money from someone for starting to settle on the land where he was born.

In any event, people are coming back, even if it is just one or two at a time for now. You can judge for yourselves what will happen under a favourable coincidence of circumstances — i.e., the adoption of a law granting every willing family a plot of land on which to set up a kin's domain.

Letter to the Russian President from Germany

ANASTASIA, reg. society
Schützlerbergerstr. 43
D-67468 Frankeneck
Tel. +49 (6325) 955-99-39
Fax +49 (6325) 18-38-59
www.anastasia-de.com
E-mail: info@anastasia-de.com
ANASTASIA, reg. society

Administrative Office,
President of the Russian Federation
Staraya ploshchad', 4, Moscow 102132

Dear President of Russia, Vladimir Vladimirovich Putin!

This is a letter from former citizens of a country which no longer exists — the USSR. For various reasons many of us find ourselves living abroad. Germany has become a refuge for more than three million former Soviet citizens. While flocking over the border and discovering the Western 'civilised Paradise', many of us have recognised that at the same time we have lost our Motherland, without which no one can ever be happy in the fullest sense.

Today in Russia a brand new idea has made its appearance, guaranteeing Man's physical and mental health, an idea already appealing to many people of various nationalities, including those living in Western Europe. Thanks to this idea, we realise that right now it is Russia that possesses the spiritual potential needed for the re-birth of harmonious Man and the restoration of a harmonious State.

Detailed information about this idea is available in the Ringing Cedars Series by Vladimir Megré, which to date has sold almost six million copies overall. It is Megré's books that have given Russians living in the Commonwealth of Independent States and other countries a new and marvellous hope of re-birth, which is a vital need for every Man, family and State.

The substance of the idea can be summed up as follows:

Every family or citizen should have the right to receive, free of charge, one hectare of land on which to set up their little Motherland, their family domain, which can be passed down by inheritance from generation to generation. Man was born on the land and should have his own specific piece of his Motherland, created and cultivated with his own hands — and the hands of several generations of his family.

In one of your speeches you stated that Russia was born and long lived in the countryside, on the land, and that that is its destined path. We agree! Having tasted the pleasures of Western civilisation, we are acutely aware that drug trafficking, prostitution, the plight of homeless children, thievery and murder, are all the fruits of this same celebrated civilisation. We are not even mentioning the most painful European problems — namely, the environment and demographics. Russia, too, has been experiencing these same problems in trying to reinvent itself on the Western model. Today it is becoming clear to many in the West that the path being followed by their democratic states is leading to a dead end, if not utter self-destruction.

Russia has gone through difficult trials over the many centuries of its history, all of which have served to nurture a special spirit among its people. It is thanks to this spirit that, at times of the most despairing spiritual and environmental crises, its citizens will be able to stand on the edge of the abyss and, in spite of everything, not only give birth to a new national idea — grow new life — but also to head off the catastrophe of self-destruction which threatens all mankind.

We, as former citizens of the USSR, are fully aware of what is meant by the simple concept of *Motherland*. Whether we have taken out foreign citizenship or not, many of us have realised that our hearts and souls remain in the places we lived for most of our lives.

We would like to return to Russia and start creating our family domains, establishing new-style communities. The activity of setting up a family domain will lead to an improvement in the quality of life for the whole commonwealth of people. We realise that a lot depends on us, on our labours, our capabilities, our experience. Many of us have taken on new professions in Europe, we have studied foreign languages, some of us have started our own businesses. There are quite a few of us who have begun studying the experience of Western eco-villages and non-traditional methods of farming.

In our communities we shall build our own schools, clubs and hospitals. There may not be a need for special government subsidies, as our numbers include all sorts of experts, and we are prepared and able to seek out our own financing and opportunities.

This kind of activity will lead to a fundamental improvement in the lives of the great commonwealth of people. Lands that have been unused, abandoned or have lain waste up 'til now, will become fruitful orchards, and on them will be born new generations of Russians with a new consciousness, with a new feeling for and outlook on the world.

Moreover, we all desire to assist our relatives and family members now living in Russia or the Commonwealth of Independent States. This will also help solve the problems faced by youth, the jobless and the homeless. We are prepared, right this moment, to muster the forces of several generations of our families, and also put all our capabilities, experience, knowledge and financial resources toward the goal of co-creating a proud, majestic and mighty Motherland of Russia.

To implement this idea we ask your consideration of the following questions:

1. Every willing family or individual citizen should be granted the right to receive, at no charge, one hectare of land for lifetime use with the right of inheritance (but with no right to sell), whereon to create a family domain.

2. Simplification of the procedures to obtain Russian citizenship on the part of those who wish to create their own little Motherland and a vast Russia, who were born on the territory of the RSFSR[28] or of other erstwhile Soviet republics and who formerly held citizenship in the USSR.

Faithfully and respectfully,

Future Citizens of Russia.

Germany, 160 signatures.

---

[28]*RSFSR* — abbreviation for *Russian Soviet Federated Socialist Republic,* i.e., the part of the USSR that after its formal disintegration became known as the Russian Federation.

This letter, unfortunately, met no reply at all from Russia. Not even a simple pro-forma memo from some kind of official was received in response. The Russian-speaking community in Germany has in their possession a postal confirmation to the effect that the Administrative Office of the Russian President indeed received their letter.

You know, this lack of response is already becoming a pattern. It's not just you, but we who are living here in Russia too, we aren't getting any reply either. On the Internet site [of the Anastasia Foundation] there is a whole section full of letters, some of them written in English, including letters addressed to the President of Russia. For five years now people have been writing on one and the same topic — kin's domains — but to date there has not been a single reply, either to individually or collectively written letters.[29]

As you will soon realise, it couldn't be any other way, since here in Russia there are forces which have pegged themselves higher than the President or the Government. They believe themselves to be higher than the people, too, only I think this is an ill-founded belief. Of course one can rise higher than a drunken people. But there is not and cannot be any power

---

[29]Even more tellingly, during President Putin's major Internet conference on 6 July 2006, over 10,000 conference participants asked or voted for questions specifically dealing with the allocation of land for kin's domains. The seven most popular questions on the topic of agriculture (which the government declares to be a high priority) were *all* about the allocation of land for kin's domains. President Putin chose to answer a wide variety of questions (including, for example, "At what age did you first have sexual intercourse?") but not a single question on kin's domains. Four days later, Russia's leading business journal *Expert* commented that this particular Internet conference served as a good indication of the most burning issues in Russian society today, and observed that allocation of land for kin's domains was among them.

higher than a people in whose hearts lives not only a dream of the future but a burning desire to put such a dream into practice.

It behooves me to respond to you, dear former fellow-citizens, on behalf of our government officials, on behalf of the President.

First of all I must thank you people, you who now live in Germany, America, Israel, Poland, the Czech Republic and Slovakia, Italy and France, Georgia, Belarus and Kazakhstan, even in Mongolia. It is thanks to your efforts that the books about Anastasia have been translated and published in the countries where you are currently residing. I didn't know you personally, and so was unable to ask you to do this. But there is something I do know. I know how your hearts have been touched and how you went about approaching publishers and translators, and when you did not find a reciprocal understanding, you set about translating and publishing my books yourselves. This happened, for example, in the Czech Republic and Slovakia, Canada and America.

And finally you found some understanding! I felt this for the first time in Germany when I addressed readers' conferences in Berlin and Stuttgart.

Sitting together in the overflowing auditorium were Russian-speakers who had emigrated to Germany from Russia and native German-speakers who had no knowledge of Russian, in roughly equal numbers. I knew the two groups didn't get along all that well. But here they were sitting side by side and good-naturedly trying to explain to one another the translation from Russian, which was, I'm sure, not always understandable.

I used to consider Germans pedantic and not a strongly emotional people. But life has shown me otherwise. It was none other than a German farmer who, after reading about Anastasia, got into his car and drove all the way to Siberia.

He went knowing neither the language nor the Russian road system, neither the Russian traffic police nor the weather. He got there. He returned home with Russian souvenirs for his friends.

My great gratitude naturally goes out to all those who at their own initiative, and sometimes at their own expense, have translated and published the books abroad. But the books, after all, are not the most important thing. Something else is. Thank you all for your understanding and support of the ideas and dream that have come out of Siberian Russia. Now this dream is no longer just a Russian dream. Now it is yours as well, and in equal measure. May you succeed in preserving it, putting it into practice and passing it on to be perfected by your children.

It is hard to tell who has performed the most significant service — Anastasia, with her impassioned sayings, the books themselves, or all those who have seized upon the idea and carried the torch forward?

Anastasia has said:

"I give the whole of my soul to people. In people I shall prevail through my soul. Prepare yourself, all wickedness and evil-mindedness, to leave the Earth...."[30]

I thought these were just simple words. However, life has shown me that they are not simple at all.

Anastasia's dream has been lit with tiny sparks in the hearts of millions of people scattered across the globe — people of many different nationalities and faiths. This dream is no longer just *her* dream. It belongs to many people and will not fade. It is now the dream of the ages and of eternity!

[30] Quoted from Book 3, Chapter 24: "Who are you, Anastasia?".

CHAPTER ELEVEN

One hectare —
a piece of Planet Earth

I'm often told: "Why do you make such a fuss over one hectare? — there are more important things." But in my view there is nothing more important in our life right now than to return the Earth to its original flourishing state.

And that is why I keep talking about a hectare of family land — behind it, after all, there is something immeasurably more significant. I don't always have the reasoning and intellectual capacity — nor, perhaps, the temperament — to explain this, but when there's even just a little breakthrough and people understand, well, I consider that a victory.

One occasion in particular stands out. The year was 2003. Switzerland. Zürich. An international forum. I was invited by the organisers and allotted a time to speak. I began talking about an idea that saw its birth in Russia, but the audience didn't appear all that receptive.

Then there was a question from the floor:

"How do you tie in this hectare of land with Man's spiritual development? Perhaps the problem of land tillage is important enough for Russia, but these questions have long been resolved in Europe. We're here to talk about spirituality."

A little nervous, I began my reply this way:

I'm talking about a hectare of land and setting up one's family domain on it, and some people might think that's a rather primitive notion. We have to talk about the great teachings on spirituality, they say, because that is the topic of this

prestigious European forum. I know — I was told by the organisers — that sitting before me in this auditorium are well-
known innovative educators, philosophers and writers on
spirituality from all over Europe, along with other thinkers
on this topic who are no less important. But it is precisely because I am mindful of the composition of this audience here
before me that I am specifically talking about a hectare of
land.

Ladies and gentlemen, I am convinced that concepts such
as love and spirituality must necessarily have a material embodiment.

The hectare of land I have in mind, the hectare Anastasia
speaks about, is much more than a mere hectare of land. It is
a Space through which you may be connected to the Cosmos.
All the planets of the Universe will react to this Space and,
consequently, to you. They will be your friends, assistants and
co-creators.

In terms of the laws of Nature, look what happens to an ordinary flower — a daisy, for example. The daisy is inseparably
connected with the Cosmos, the planets and the Sun. The
flower opens its petals when the Sun comes up, and closes
them when the Sun goes down. They are at one with each
other, in harmony with each other. Not even trillions of kilometres or light-years could break the connection. They are
bonded together — the great Sun and the little earthly flower.
They know that only together can they be creators of a great
universal harmony.

But every single blade of grass on the Earth reacts not only
to the Sun. It also reacts to other planets. It reacts to Man,
to the energy of his feelings.

Scientists conducted an experiment in which sensors were
attached to an ordinary flowering house-plant, and polygraph
indicators registered even the minutest energy impulses coming from the flower. Several people were sent into the room

in turn. One of them simply walked past the flower, a second went over and gave it some water, while a third went in and cut off one of the leaves. According to the data registered by the polygraph, whenever the person who tore off a leaf entered the room, the plant would get agitated and cause the indicator to jump.[1]

A related phenomenon can also be often noticed: flowers fade when their owner goes away. The upshot is, that all plants react to Man. They may like a particular Man or they may not. Consequently, they may transmit to their planets a message of either love or absence of love.

And now imagine that you have some kind of Space — say, a hectare of land. This isn't just any run-of-the-mill hectare of land where potatoes are grown for sale, but a hectare of land on which you have begun to create, based on a particular level of consciousness or spirituality.

You have your own territory on which there are a whole lot of plants cultivated not by hired workers, but directly by you yourself. Every plant, every blade of grass will react to you with love, and these plants, as living beings, are capable of collecting for you all the best energies of the Universe. They collect them and offer them to you. Plants feed on more than just the energy of the soil. After all, you are aware that there are some plants that can grow even without soil.

Five thousand years ago in Ancient Egypt there lived priests who created a variety of religions. And these priests were in control of whole nations. These priests were the richest people in the world of that time. The basements of their palaces

---

[1]This is apparently a reference to the research conducted by the American polygraph scientist Cleve Backster (1924–). For further information see Cleve Backster's *Primary perception: Biocommunication with plants, living foods, and human cells* (Anza, California: White Rose Millennium Press, 2003) or Peter Tompkins and Christopher Bird's *The secret life of plants* (New York: Harper & Row, 1973), esp. Chapter 1: "Plants and ESP".

were filled with trunks of gold and precious gems. They were acquainted with a whole range of secret sciences. The pharaoh turned to them for advice and money.

But each of these highly placed priests had his own hectare of land, on which he permitted no slaves to work. These were the richest people of their day, with a knowledge of a great many sciences. They knew the secrets of a hectare of land. On the walls of the ancient temples of Egypt, the priests' temples, was inscribed the warning: *Do not accept food from a slave.* This is Example One.

Example Two. In Ancient Rome the senators issued a decree that if a slave was capable of working on the land and had been given land, then that slave could be sold to another master only if the land were sold with him, so as not to let any outsiders into contact with what was growing on that land. And why did the Roman senators give land to some of their slaves? And why did they give them money on top of that to build themselves a house? For one reason only: to obtain ten percent of a harvest which had been cultivated and nurtured with love and care by the Man growing it. It was only produce like this that could be at all beneficial.

The Egyptian priests and the senators of Ancient Rome knew what kind of food was beneficial to Man. The produce we eat today is in no way fit for human consumption — it's 'dead produce'. There is a vast difference between berries one picks from a bush to eat on the spot and berries sold in a supermarket. It's not just that they've already started to decay, but there's no energy left in them. They are incapable of feeding Man's soul. And I'm not even mentioning the mutant plants created by our technological world.

So, if you don't have your own hectare of land, there's nowhere that you're going to find food worthy of human consumption. You can take a little money and buy some sort of vegetables. But you must realise that those vegetables were not grown for you. They weren't grown for any Man at all. They were grown for money.

There is not a disease which cannot be cured by the Space of Love — a Space you have created with your own hands and your own soul.

People are the children of God. The world of animals and plants, the air and the Space around us — these are also God's creations. And everything taken together is nothing less than the materially embodied spirit of God. If someone calls himself a highly spiritual person, let him show the material embodiment of his spirituality.

Imagine God looking down on you from above right now. And He sees someone driving a tram, another one of His children constructing buildings, another standing in a store and selling things from behind a counter. These aren't the professions God created. They're professions for slaves. God didn't want his children to be slaves. And He created a marvellous world and gave it in stewardship to His children. Take care of it and use it! But to do that, you must understand this world. Understand what the Moon is, what the herb known as the yarrow is...

And what is a hectare of land? Is it a place where Man must work by the sweat of his brow? *No!* It is a place where Man shouldn't work at all. It is a place through which Man ought to control the world. Tell me, who gives greater pleasure to God — a Man driving a tram or a Man who might have only a small piece of land but has transformed it into a Paradise? The latter, of course.

Can people today open up a road to the Cosmos? Or can they be taught how to settle the Moon or Mars? Of course not! Because they'll put weapons and pollution there, and end up having the same wars there as on the Earth. Yet Man, after all, has been created to populate other worlds. And this will come about only when Man understands and beautifies his own Earth. The way to settle the planets of the Universe isn't technical at all, it is psychotelepathic.

Man needs to become consciously aware of what constitutes the true beauty of the Universe.

Your city of Zürich is considered beautiful. We can say a thousand times how beautiful it is. But what, specifically, is beautiful about it? Yes, it is very clean here. Yes, it looks as though there are many well-to-do people living here. But is land covered with asphalt truly beautiful? Is it really good to have little green islands popping up just in certain places? Is it good that there's a dying tree — a majestic cedar — right in the centre of your city? It's suffocating from the smog. It's suffocating from exhaust fumes. And it's not the only thing that's dying and suffocating. The people walking along the city streets are suffocating from these fumes too.

We should give some thought to all that we have managed to contrive on this Earth. And it's best to talk about it in very simple terms. Let each one of us take a small plot of his land, pull his whole mind and whole spirituality together and create a very small but concrete Paradise. He will transform his little piece of land on our large planet into a flourishing garden, giving a material embodiment to his spirituality, following God's example. If millions of people do this in a whole lot of countries, then the whole Earth will become a flourishing garden, and there won't be any wars, because millions of people will be completely engaged in a grand co-creation. And if Russians should then descend upon Switzerland or Germany, it will only be to delight in the contemplation of beautiful living oases, to learn from their experience in embodying true spirituality.

Russia, unfortunately, is currently trying with all its might to be like the West. Russia's politicians are peppering their speeches with references to Western countries as *developed* or *civilised*. They are urging their people to catch up to them in 'development' and 'being civilised'. Our politicians still don't know that we have the opportunity not only to catch up quickly, but to significantly overtake them. But this can come to pass only if Russia does a complete about-face and starts heading in the opposite direction.

This is in no way to suggest I am trying to denigrate or insult your Western civilisation. But we're talking here, after all, about spirituality, and we need to be honest and sincere in what we say to one another. Spirituality cannot be measured simply by material wealth and technological achievements. Such a one-sided, technocratic approach to mankind's development will invariably lead to an abyss. No doubt those of you gathered here today will admit this, but then you must also admit that you are running out in front, with us right behind you. Try to stop and figure out what's happened to our world. If you do manage to figure it out, call out to those running behind you: *Hey, you'd better stop, chaps! Stop running! There's an abyss ahead, and we're already on the edge of it. Find another way.*

If we really listen to our hearts, together, we ought to go from simply talking about spirituality to its material embodiment. One hectare is but a tiny dot on the face of our planet Earth. But millions of these dots will transform the whole planet into a flourishing garden. Trillions of flower petals, along with the happy smiles of children and oldsters will tell the Universe that the people of the Earth are ready for a grand co-creation.

And the planets of the Universe will respond:

"We're waiting for you, Man. We're waiting for you, worthy son of God!"

Our millennium has ushered in a great transformation on the Earth. Tens of thousands of Russian families have already aspired to obtain their own hectare of land. A father and mother who are actually creating a Space of Love for their children are more spiritual than the most celebrated wise-men who only *talk* about spirituality.

Let the spirit of each Man spring up from the ground as a beautiful flower, a tree with fragrant fruit, and let this take place on every single hectare of our planet.

After these words, for some time absolute silence reigned in the hall. This was followed by thunderous applause.

I spoke in Zürich on the following day, too. Once again, to a full house. A number of our former compatriots were present here, too.

I don't think I came across too coherently, especially since I was speaking through an interpreter. But people stayed, they listened, because it wasn't just me that was talking with this audience — a higher power was speaking. A very simple, specific, yet at the same time extraordinary, power, one that has been preserved for millennia in the depths of the human soul — a nostalgia for the true way of life for Man as Creator.

And then I thought: *Do I really need to explain to anyone that all Russia's sons and daughters that have been blown away by an ill wind will most definitely return? Of course they'll come back!* You will remember Anastasia's words:[2]

Mother Russia will greet crowds of guests on that day! They are all of the Earth as Atlanteans born! As prodigal sons they shall return. Let all the bards everywhere play on their guitars. And the old shall write letters to their children. And children to their parents. Both you and I shall become very young, and people will feel young for the very first time.

[2]Quoted (approximately) from Book 2, Chapter 9: "Dachnik Day and an All-Earth holiday!".

CHAPTER TWELVE

People power

There is one additional question I would like to bring to my readers' attention.

At the moment you are engaged in the process of creating a people's strategy for the future development of the Russian State. Part of this strategy has been published in issues of the almanac,[1] part appears on the Anastasia site on the Internet. As I see it, the overwhelming majority of the materials is extremely interesting. However there is one question — about power and authority — that has not yet been sufficiently illuminated. Yet it is a most important question. I invite you to join me in contemplating it. For starters, I'd like to share my own reasonings with you.

Power often changes. Just over the past hundred years, people have lived under the Tsar, the Communists and a series of democratic rulers. Power gets changed, but life does not get rearranged for the better. Why? Do bad people always come to power? Hardly. It is more likely that the current system makes any politicians who get elected to power ineffective pen-pushers when it comes to solving the problems involved in any real betterment of people's lives.

Take our legislative assemblies over the most recent parliamentary terms. It seems that we vote for normal, family-type people, and then once they're in power they come up with, to put it mildly, some rather strange legislation. Why? Perhaps,

---

[1] *the almanac* — see footnote 1 in Book 7, Chapter 28: "To the readers of the Ringing Cedars Series".

in the process of coming to power, they fall into another world — a world isolated from the people? An apartment in the parliamentary living quarters, a car equipped with its own flashing light on top, a private office where the public is denied entry, along with all sorts of special perks and "vanity of vanities".

Anastasia's Grandfather suggested an interesting piece of draft legislation concerning deputies of the State Duma. They should each be granted a piece of land and definitely live in a community built on that land, right out among the people. A law faculty graduate in Ukraine named Tatiana Borodina,[2] has drafted a bill to this effect, and I think it is worth reproducing its major clauses here in this book, so that my readers can pass on the proposal to their own elected representatives in legislative assemblies at all levels.

Moreover, I call upon my readers to be sure to take part in regional and federal elections, but to vote in only those candidates who live in their own kin's domains.

But is it merely a passport stamp that defines someone as a Russian citizen? In many cases, a candidate on the ballot has Russian citizenship and a Moscow residence permit, but has a fashionable domain located in another country. Is he going to be mindful of the needs of ordinary Russian people? Most probably his thoughts will be oriented in a completely different direction.

If a candidate has his own little Motherland — his family domain in Russia — and lives there among Russian citizens, his work can be expected to bring benefit to those citizens and to the Motherland as a whole.

This much is becoming clear to many people. Students are even beginning to draft laws to assist the legislators.

---

[2]*Tatiana Borodina* — see reference in Chapter 10 ("*The Book of Kin* and *A Family Chronicle*") above, especially footnote 19.

A law of Russia on Family Communities created by Russian People's Deputies on all levels (draft)

The law defines the legal, social and economic provisions for the creation and maintenance of Family Communities and Family Domains on the part of Russian People's Deputies,[3] thereby guaranteeing the right of Russian citizens — as proclaimed in Russia's Constitution — to hold land as the foundation for the wealth of the nation.

The law is aimed at the creation of favourable working conditions for Russian People's Deputies, conducive to the development, drafting and adoption of federal legislation, as well as guaranteeing their maximum contact with voters.

Article 1. Basic terms and concepts used in the Law

Certain specific terms used in the Law are defined as follows:

• *Family Domain* — a plot of land from 1 to 1.3 hectares in size, granted to age-of-majority Russian citizens for their lifetime use, with the right of inheritance, with no tax obligations in respect to the land or its produce;

• *Family Community* — a centre of population organised on the principles of local self-government, consisting of Family Domains as well as socio-cultural and community facilities;

• *lifetime use* — unconditional ownership and use of a plot of land, free of charge and in perpetuity;

---

[3]*Russian People's Deputies* (Russian: *Narodnye deputaty Rossii*) — formal title of elected political representatives (members of parliament or a governing council) at the federal, regional and local levels.

• *living fence* — a hedge consisting of trees and shrubs planted around the perimeter of a Family Domain or a Family Community.

Article 2. Legislation on Family Domains and Family Communities

The procedures involved in granting a Russian People's Deputy an allotment of land for the creation of a Family Community, as well as the definition of the legal status of Family Domains and Family Communities and their functions, are all governed by the Russian Constitution, the Russian Land Code, this Law, the Russian Law on Family Domains and Family Communities, as well as other applicable laws.

Article 3. Basic principles of legislation governing Family Communities

The creation of Family Communities by Russian People's Deputies is subject to the following basic principles:

(a) compliance with the law;

(b) the setting of conditions for the implementation by all Russian citizens of their right to hold land as the foundation for the wealth of the nation;

(c) the principle that ownership and use of the plot of land granted for the creation of a Family Domain shall be free of charge, unconditional and in perpetuity;

(d) exemption of the owner of a Family Domain from payment of taxes on the sale of produce grown or goods produced on said Family Domain;

(e) the creation of one Family Community by one Russian People's Deputy of the current parliamentary term;

(f) other applicable principles.

Article 4. Purview of the Law

The purview of this Law covers Russian People's Deputies at all levels of government who are elected in accordance with

electoral laws, as well as age-of-majority Russian citizens who
have expressed a desire to live in a Family Community organised on the principles set forth in this Law.

Article 5. Granting an allotment of land to a Russian People's Deputy for the creation of a Family Community

1. Each Russian People's Deputy serving a current or future term, within a year from the date of his election, shall be
granted an allotment of land at least 150 ha in size whereon to
establish a Family Community (hereinafter: *land allotment*).

2. Upon election as a Russian People's Deputy under the
proportional system from a political party's or a party-alli-
ance's candidates' list in a nation-wide election, the successful candidate shall be granted a land allotment in a region of
Russia of his choosing.

Upon election as a Russian People's Deputy by a majority
of voters in a single-representative electoral district, the successful candidate shall be granted a land allotment on the territory of the district where he is elected.

3. A single Family Community shall not be created by two
or more Russian People's Deputies, neither shall two or more
Russian People's Deputies be permitted to live in the same
Family Community during the same term of office.

4. The land allotment is granted as a single parcel of land
(including any water resources thereon) from properties belonging to the State or already held communally. Land may
also be expropriated from people making full-time use of it
and transferred to a Russian People's Deputy for the creation
of a Family Community.

5. If required, land may be purchased from property owners for community needs, in which case the property owner
must be given a minimum of a year's notice in writing by the
respective decision-making body, and must also give his own
consent to the sale. The purchase price is to be determined

by an expert's assessment of the land's monetary value, which is to be carried out in accordance with the methodology established by the federal Cabinet.

6. A plot of land recommended for inclusion in the land allotment for the creation of a Family Community by a Russian People's Deputy, but which is in the possession of a physical or legal person, may, with the agreement of the property owner, be exchanged for another plot of land of equal value — either in the same region or in another region of Russia, depending on the property owner's preference.

7. Russian citizens who own plots of land or shares in 'real' (individually registered) plots of land adjacent to the territory of a proposed Family Community, have the right to reassign their properties, without monetary payment, for the purposes of creating a Family Community by a Russian People's Deputy, and receive in return a plot of land within said Community, whereon to create a Family Domain for their lifetime use.

8. A Russian citizen who owns 'virtual' shares in communal (not individually registered) plots of land, has the right to transfer his shares, either wholly or in part (no less than 1 ha in size) for the purposes of creating a Family Community by a Russian People's Deputy, and receive in return a plot of land within said Community, whereon to create a Family Domain for his lifetime use.

Article 6. Land composition in Family Communities

1. The land in a Family Community is comprised of the following types of plots:
• land plots for the creation of a Family Domain;
• land plots for the creation of Family Domains on the part of children of a Russian People's Deputy (no more than two plots per Community).

2. Land plots reserved for socio-cultural and community purposes are designated in accordance with the overall plan

of the Family Community. The aggregate of such plots is not to exceed 7% of the total area of the Community. The said plots are under the jurisdiction of the Local Council of the said Family Community.

3. The remaining portion of the land allotment is to be divided into plots of land for the creation of Family Domains of no less than 1 ha each. The size may be extended to 1.3 ha depending on the peculiarities of the terrain and other pertinent factors.

4. Between all land plots walkways must be created, no less than 3 or 4 metres wide. Each plot owner has the right to plant a living fence around the perimeter of his Family Domain.

5. On plots of land designated for the creation of a Family Domain, Russian citizens have the right to plant trees and shrubs (including those of the forest variety), to create artificial reservoirs, construct houses and outbuildings and erect ancillary structures and other facilities, provided principles of good-neighbourliness are observed.

Article 7. Order of distribution of land plots designated for the creation of Family Domains among Russian citizens

1. In the proposed Family Communities the Russian People's Deputies have the right to be the first to select for themselves one land plot for the creation of a Family Domain for their lifetime use with right of inheritance.

2. Each child of a Russian People's Deputy with a family of his own has the right to receive a land plot for the creation of a Family Domain for his lifetime use.

3. It is mandatory that one or two land plots in the Family Community be granted to refugees or to children from orphanages.

4. Russian People's Deputies, at their discretion, have the right to grant to Russian citizens of their choosing up to 30% of the remaining land plots, whereon said citizens are to create their own Family Domains.

5. The remaining land plots should be given to Russian citizens belonging to a variety of social classes (entrepreneurs, social workers, pensioners, representatives of the creative intelligentsia, military personnel etc.). Land plots are to be distributed among Russian citizens on the basis of a lottery conducted openly at a general meeting of future residents of each Family Community.

Article 8. Local Councils of Family Communities

1. The Local Council of each Family Community comprises those living in said Community, united by the fact of their permanent residence within the boundaries of said Community, which constitutes a self-contained administrative-territorial entity.

2. The Local Council of the Family Community has the right to create a representative organ of local self-government, namely, the Family Community Council, whose members are drawn exclusively from among the residents of the said Community.

3. Russian People's Deputies are prohibited from standing for election or being elected to the Family Community Council. In cases where a Russian People's Deputy is elected to a Family Community Council, their election shall be declared null and void.

4. The procedures for setting up local self-government are regulated by the By-laws of the Local Council of the Family Community (hereinafter: *By-laws*), which said Council has the right to adopt at one of its meetings or by a local referendum. The By-laws must be registered with the district office of the Ministry of Justice.

Article 9. Status of land plots in respect to creating a Family Domain

1. Plots of land designated for the creation of Family Domains are granted — for lifetime use with the right of inheritance —

only to citizens of Russia. It is forbidden to grant land plots for Family Domains to citizens of foreign countries or to state-less persons, except those who have been granted legal refugee status (but no more than two such families are permitted per Family Community created by a Russian People's Deputy).[*]

I don't know how much time I had spent walking around while Anastasia's grandfather familiarised himself with the contents of the documents I had brought with me[4] when all of a sudden I heard a loud and raucous outburst of laughter, which sounded not at all like that of an old man. He was still laughing when I dashed over to him.

"That's rich!... Oho, that really makes me laugh!... Thank you... Thank you, Vladimir! And to think I didn't want to get into these at first!"

"But now that you are into them, what's so funny? After all, this is a most serious situation! And an extremely compli-cated one!"

"Extremely complicated for whom?" Grandfather asked.

"For me and for my readers wishing to build the domains Anastasia talked about."

[*] A detailed draft and commentary will be published in a forthcoming regu-lar issue of the *Ringing Cedars of Russia* almanac, which you will be able to purchase. It would be a good idea for readers to bring this to the attention of Russian People's Deputies at all levels of government. — *Footnote from the original Russian edition.*

[4] See the beginning of Chapter 9 above.

Quite possibly in uttering these words I might have sounded irritated and hurt. Grandfather stopped laughing, looked at me intently and replied quietly and seriously:

"To this day I cannot understand why my granddaughter would have anything to do with you, let alone bear children with you. Only don't be mad at this old man, Vladimir. Maybe I don't get it, which means others too may not get it, but it's possible that in this 'not getting it' lies a great truth. And so I don't have any bad feelings toward you. And I don't condemn my granddaughter. On the contrary, I'm very excited about what's been achieved."

"But is there anything specific you have to say about the contents of these documents?"

"I've already said it — I'm excited about what's been achieved."

"By whom?"

"By my granddaughter."

"But I was asking you about what I'd written."

Grandfather looked first at the packet of documents and then, silently and intently, at me, before replying.

"I really can't say, Vladimir, just how necessary your appeal to the public really is. Maybe it is indeed important for them. As I see it, what I read simply confirms that even back ten years ago my granddaughter foresaw all these ups and downs, and long ago everything that seems to be working against you she's turned into something beneficial."

"How can you call offending my readers and me *beneficial*?"

"Did you realise *who's* been offending you and your readers?"

"Some kind of entity that's set itself up under the cover of Russia's Orthodox Church."

"And it provoked a feeling in you of being offended?"

"Yeah."

"Well, that's good! Now it's not just with your mind, but with the feelings that you and many of your readers have experienced, that you can understand how your forebears were defamed in the eyes of their descendants — how they were called pagans and for centuries were blamed for all sorts of misdeeds they never committed. You're not the only one who's tried to write about this. There have been quite a few historians over the centuries who have tried to refute this slander — but in vain.

"What's happening now is that the same tactics are being used all over again to discredit people who really want to reach out and touch God's creations. There are quite a few of these people now, and they can feel by their own experience how their forebears were smeared like that. The souls of their distant ancestors are finding renewed strength through those being slandered in our time. Their forebears of yesterday will act like guardian angels, protecting their descendants of today.

"Believe me, there can be no kinder and brighter force — no way — than that which is emerging in the world right now. If this is coming about for people today — if some invisible thread is capable of joining today's son together with his parent who lived two thousand years ago — and if the thread that joins them together can be extended, then today's Man will be joined together with God, his original Parent."

Grandfather was clearly trying to restrain his excitement as he told me this. But I felt I needed further clarification.

"Maybe what you say is very important," I observed. "But, you see, there's been quite a bit of delay with the creation of family domains."

"But, just maybe, such a delay is necessary to give people the opportunity to figure things out and co-create a design for the future?"

"Maybe. It's all turning out rather unexpectedly. As though the first book began with just simple actions, then with the second came readers' clubs, and now, with *The Book of Kin* out, the *Family Chronicle* has come along."

These words made Grandfather laugh again, but he immediately cut himself short, and said with a kindly smile:

"My granddaughter was clearly having a fun time with that *Family Chronicle*! Maybe it was to comfort you and your readers somehow. But hey, look how she arranged it so that Russia's supreme rulers and the Patriarch of the Church supported her idea! Even if it's just *one* of her ideas. No mention of her philosophy, or maybe they simply didn't understand it. Their names will not go down in the annals of old — they're too wishy-washy, not very bold.

"People will be eternally remembered in the annals of old who are right now, at least in their thoughts, creating their own God-pleasing domains. Whether they themselves chose the idea or whether it chose them, that doesn't matter any more. Eternity awaits those who are co-creating a future for their children — and not just for their children but for themselves too. For the first time on the Earth, Man who is born for eternity will come back to eternity.

"Vladimir, I'm just beginning to understand my granddaughter's achievements. It is possible that many secrets of life have been revealed to her. But there is one which even the high priests were not fully aware of. All they ever knew before was that human life *could* be eternal. Part of this knowledge allowed them, for example, to be reincarnated over and over. But this reincarnation was never complete. And this is why their achievements did not bring joy either to themselves or to mankind.

"Now I am confident — and believe me — that Anastasia has full knowledge of the creations needed to attain eternity. You might ask her about this and try to understand. And if she can come up with words that a great many people will understand, worlds worthy of a god-Man will be unfurled to their thought.

"Take a walk over to my granddaughter, Vladimir, and have a talk with her. At the moment she is sitting under the cedar, down by the lakeshore. There may be significant revealings in the world all around when the words of eternity are found which are comprehensible to both mind and feelings. The aspirations of the great awakened civilisation will whirl upward. The whole galaxy will feel these great aspirations and will await with shivers of anticipation the touch of those capable of giving to the planets a new and marvellous life. Go, and be not slow."

I had already taken several steps when I was stopped by Anastasia's grandfather crying out:

"Vladimir, it's high time that you and Anastasia's followers started your own Motherland party."

"A party? What kind of party?"

"I'm telling you! That's what you should call it — the *Motherland Party*!"[5]

---

[5]*Motherland Party* (Russian: *Rodnaya Partiya*) — Following the publication of this appeal, several groups of inspired readers and sponsors did set about establishing the proposed 'Motherland Party'. However, since Vladimir Megré subsequently changed his mind and decided to align himself with the *Edinaya Rossiya* (One Russia) Party, loyal to the existing régime of Vladimir Putin (and invited his followers to follow suit), the proposed party never got off the ground, and Megré's move caused some dissension among his followers.

CHAPTER THIRTEEN

A new civilisation

Anastasia was sitting beneath the cedar tree, wearing a light grey flaxen dress. With her arms around her knees and her head slightly lowered, she was gazing out at the smooth surface of the lake. I didn't go up to her right away. For a while I stood at a distance, observing this recluse quietly sitting there by the lakeshore. No — that description really doesn't fit Anastasia. The word *recluse* is better suited to the people who live in modern apartments.

People live in these apartments and don't even know their neighbours sharing the same floor.[1] They walk along the street and couldn't care less about the people they meet. And their attitude is entirely reciprocal.

So, while there's nothing frightening in someone living alone, it's a lot more frightening when they're alone amongst people like themselves.

And so, even though Anastasia was sitting here alone on the shore of this taiga lake, her heart was beating in unison with millions of human hearts all over the world. Some call her their friend, some their sister, feeling like they're related to her.

---

[1] In contrast with North American practice, Russian apartment blocks, even the ones that appear massive from the outside, are usually divided into vertical sections, each with its own exterior entrance, stairs and lift (elevator). A given section might have four to six flats per floor around the stairwell and lift shaft. Hence there would not be very many "neighbours sharing the same floor".

In the meantime, her soft-spoken words wing their way through the endless flow of information thundering and dundering from TV screens and a host of other media. Her words waft by and people pick them up. And people who catch them may respond with guitar strings and songs, and often with actions. They retune their life anew.

And Grandfather... I saw for the first time how fervently he expressed himself as he asked me to have a word with Anastasia about eternity.

I sat down beside her and she turned her head toward me. I felt a calming sense from the tender gaze of her greyish-blue eyes. For a time we simply sat and looked at each other.

I couldn't help myself, but took her hand, gave it a quick kiss and then replaced it on her knees. Her cheeks were aflush with a soft glow, her eyelashes all aflutter. And without rhyme or reason a sense of unease came over me. How strange to feel uneasy over a woman one has known for ten years! And how delightful!

And in an attempt to overcome my sense of awkwardness and unease, I broke the silence first.

"I was talking with your grandfather just now, Anastasia. For some reason he quite unexpectedly and rather excitedly started saying something about humanity's need for words on eternity. He said these words should be the kind people can grasp not just with their mind or intellect, but with their feelings. Are these words really that important?"

"Yes, they are important, Vladimir. But it is not the words that are important, but, rather, people's conscious awareness. Words, of course, are necessary to bring it forth. A conscious awareness of eternal life will help perfect Man's way of life."[2]

---

[2]As noted earlier (footnote 7 in Chapter 9: "A fine state of affairs!"), the Russian phrase for 'way of life' is literally: 'image of life' (*obraz zhizni*).

"But what connection is there between our way of life and becoming consciously aware of eternity?"

"A direct connection. People today believe that they have only a few decades to live, after which they must leave life behind and disappear into oblivion. Yet all along, Man's life can be eternal. This must be brought out, so that everyone, or, at least, most people, may understand."

"But you talked about that already. And I've included your words on this subject in several of my books."

"Yes, I did, but, evidently, what I said has not been understood, or the frailty of human existence has been drummed into people's consciousness too strongly over the millennia. New words and arguments must be found."

"So, can you try to find them?"

"I shall try. We need to look for them, apparently, along with those who will understand."

"But tell me in your own words first."

"Fine. Perhaps we should put it this way...

"Most people living on the Earth believe that they plan out their own life. They choose a profession, start a family, have children or, alternatively, decline to have children. But in many respects their decisions are not their own. A great influence is exercised upon them by somebody else's will, acting through public opinion.

"For example, you have an object called a *clothes hanger*. At one point somebody decided to perfect this object by using Man himself as a clothes hanger. This gave rise to the profession you call *modelling*, from the word *model*. It is not an enviable profession, it is not part of Man's destiny.

"But somebody decided to make it one of the most attractive professions of all, and did so. They began to show off live models in a variety of colour magazine photos and TV shows, and to describe their supposedly happy lives — to tell about all the money they make and how rich people want to marry them. Millions of young girls began to dream of becoming the world's next top model and thereby attaining happiness.

"Millions of young girls all over the world began resorting to all sorts of measures in an effort to achieve this illusory glory. One in a million made it as a famous model, essentially becoming a walking clothes hanger. The others experienced deep disappointment in their lives, as their dream was not fulfilled.

"And this was due to their failure to determine their own destiny — they had begun structuring their lives under the influence of somebody else's will.

"There are many other examples that could be cited of men and women, and even children, chasing illusory values, neglecting their own purpose and destiny.

"Tell me what you think, Vladimir — if human society is made up of people like that, where can it be heading?"

"It's heading nowhere, that kind of human society. Out there, in our country — Russia — not a single political party nor the state as a whole has put forth any kind of programme for building the future. From what you have told me, Anastasia, I'm particularly interested in the definition of Man's purpose and destiny. What does it consist of? How can people discover it?"

"Let your thought, Vladimir, as well as other people's thoughts, try to grasp hold of God's creations, His programme, His dream."

"But is that really possible — grasping hold of God's dream, I mean?"

"It *is* possible. After all, He has hid nothing, and still hides nothing from people — from children who are His very own. He has written no scholarly tomes — everything by example He has shown. And the first thing everyone needs to understand and feel is which of Man's deeds to eternity lead. Think for yourself, Vladimir, why did not God, who created the living and multifaceted world, not create things like the car, the TV and the space ship in their present form?"

"Perhaps He simply wasn't up to the job, whereas Man is?"

"God created everything Man needs — Man has within himself a means of transportation as well as imagination through which he can see far better pictures than are shown on TV. Man is also capable of effecting the mastery of other planets of the Universe without the aid of primitive artificial projectiles.

"It was God who determined Man's purpose and destiny, as well as the programme of development for all life in the Universe. To attain the required understanding, Man needs to refrain from destroying His programme and to study for all he's worth and ascertain the purpose of everything on the Earth."

Immortality

"God created Man immortal. To witness this, only three conditions are required to be observed:

"*First:* create a living Space which will attract Man to itself and to which Man has aspired.

"*Second:* there should be, somewhere on the Earth, at least one person who thinks of you with kindness and love.

"*Third:* never even admit the thought that you can be overtaken by death — and this is extremely important. Even if you suggest to someone who is simply falling asleep that he is dying and he believes it, then he will die, in obedience to his thought. But even if an elderly man (in Earth terms) wears out his body and is lying at death's door, but does not think about death, but pictures his life in the living Space he has been creating, he will be born anew — such is the law of the Universe. The Universe will not stand by and allow a life-creating thought to die.

"You have a concept in your world known as *natural selection*. Even now God's programme is selecting the best of everything for a re-embodiment. Before, however, there was not much to choose from. Now it is showing a multifold increase. Whoever builds a domain with love will be reincarnated again and again.

"Whatever interferes with them will disappear from the Earth for ever, giving way to the birth of a new civilisation."

"But why a new civilisation," I asked, "if the people are going to be the same, with the same vegetation and the same planet?"

"The new civilisation, Vladimir, will be characterised by a new conscious awareness as well as by new perceptions of the surrounding world. This great principle, that has been given birth in people today, will remain invisible to ordinary sight until the appearance of the planet known as the Earth has changed. It will affect life in the Universe as a whole."

"But how can the Universe change as a result of the Earth's appearance?"

"It can, Vladimir. Even though our planet is but a small particle, it is in close interaction with other parts of the Universe. Even if one small particle should change, its changes can influence the whole spectrum of the Universe."

"Most interesting. But couldn't you show me, Anastasia, a scene from the future as to how the Universe might change?"

"I can indeed. Take a look."

Love creating worlds

Spring was in full bloom on the planet Arreta.[3] Herbs very similar to those on the Earth, along with flowers on trees and bushes, were giving off their sweet scent. A young man named Vladislav[4] was walking along a pathway amidst the springtime splendour, on his way to a symposium. He was to give a talk on the origins of life on the planet Arreta. His debating opponent would be his childhood friend Radomir.[5]

At nineteen years old, Vladislav had an adequate store of data to defend his theory before scholars at any level. But the knowledge possessed by his friend Radomir was no less in scope. Radomir and his team would pounce on any weak points or unsupported reasoning in Vladislav's arguments regarding events in the past.

Liudmila[6] would be there, too. Liudmila... As it happened, both lads had been in love with this girl right from childhood. They loved her, but never admitted it either to each other or to the girl. Instead, they were waiting for Liudmila herself to give some kind of indication as to whom she preferred.

[3] *Arreta* — The Russian name here is actually *Yalmeza,* derived from the word *Zemlya* (Earth), spelt backwards.

[4] *Vladislav* — a common Russian masculine name, originally meaning '[born] in love and glory' (although often associated with the meaning 'ruler of praise'). The subsequent variant *Vadichek* is an endearing form of this name.

[5] *Radomir* — a Russian masculine name, derived from the words *rad* ('joyful') and *mir* ('peace').

[6] *Liudmila* — a common Russian feminine name, derived from the roots *liud* ('people') and *mil* ('dear').

Vladislav had deliberately chosen a roundabout route to where the symposium was being held, in order to give more thought to his presentation. But something was interfering with his concentration. He had the impression that somebody was watching him. Upon hearing a rustle behind him, he did a sharp about-face. Someone darted from the path into the bushes and was lying still in the tall grasses. Vladislav took a few steps back the way he had come and caught sight of a figure hiding in the grasses under a bush. It was his four-year-old sister Katya.[7]

"So, Katerinka, you've latched onto me again, eh?" Vladislav tenderly addressed his sister. "I've got an important presentation coming up. Maybe you don't realise it, but you're getting in the way. Or maybe you do realise it — otherwise you wouldn't be hiding there in the grasses."

"I'm not hiding, I'm just lying here," replied Katya. "I'm looking at this flower, and all the different little bugs." And she made it look as though she really were interested in a particular little flower.

"Well, now! Then you can just go on lying there looking at them. I'm off."

Katya jumped up at once and ran over to Vladislav.

"Go ahead, Vadichek," she started rattling off. "I'll follow you ever so quietly, so's not to interfere with your thinking. When we get to the place where all the people are, you take me by the hand so that everyone can see what a handsome and clever big brother I have!"

"Okay. Don't try to sweet-talk me. Here, give me your hand. Only remember, when I or somebody else is presenting, don't even think of criticising what the grown-ups say, like last time."

---

[7]*Katya* — an endearing form of the feminine name *Yekaterina,* derived from the Greek word *katharós* ('pure'); related to 'Catherine' in English. The subsequent variant *Katerinka* conveys a hint of brotherly condescension.

Katerinka, now satisfied, grasped hold of Vladislav's hand and promised:

"I shall try with all my might not to criticise."

Representatives of the different regions of the planet Arreta, both young and old, filled the natural amphitheatre. Nobody carried pens, notepads or any kind of writing materials. Their natural memory allowed them to memorise what they heard down to the minutest detail. Vladislav carried no exhibits with him as he walked out on stage. With just the power of his thought he would be able to create holograms in space to show any scenes from the past he wished, or reproduce household objects or even feelings.

With just a hint of uneasiness, Vladislav began his presentation:

The planet on which we live is called Arreta. It is more than ninety sextillion years old. But life began here no more than three hundred years ago. For originating life here we are indebted to our forebears, two inhabitants of the planet Earth. To put it more specifically, the originating of life on the planet Arreta was due to the influence of the energy of love and the dream of two inhabitants of the planet Earth. For this reason I offer you some historical information about life on the planet Earth.

The earliest period of people's life on Earth was quite possibly similar to our own. They had a good knowledge and feeling of their planet and the purpose of the Universe.

Earth-dwellers determined the purpose of all the living organisms of their planet, and made efficient use of them.

But one day a disaster occurred. The consciousness of one of the Earth's inhabitants was invaded by a virus which soon spread intensively among the other inhabitants of the planet. Our scientists have termed this virus *death*.

The outward signs of this virus, as indicated by historical records, are characterised as follows. The people infected by it start to destroy their own perfect variety of life on the planet, creating in its place a primitive, artificial world. This period of life Earth-dwellers themselves referred to as the *technocratic age*.

The people infected by the death virus began mutating from rational beings into anti-rational beings. They gathered together in large numbers on small plots of land and built themselves dwellings that looked like stone tombs, piled one on top of another.

Picture to yourselves a stone mountain with a whole lot of burrows hollowed out in it. It was something quite similar to these stone mountains that people built with their hands and called *apartment blocks*. The tomb-burrows in this artificial mountain were called *apartments*. A massive concentration of these artificial stone mountains with their burrows, piled up one beside the other, was called a *city*.

These so-called cities were filled with air unfit to breathe and water unfit to drink, along with stale food. Even during Earth-dwellers' lifetime, various organs of the human anatomy would begin to decay and decompose. Of course it is difficult to imagine human bodies walking around containing decaying and decomposing organs. But that's exactly how it was.

Historical sources indicate that people of the technocratic age even had a science they called *medicine*. They considered one of the big achievements of this science to be the ability to replace their internal organs. People did not understand that the very existence of such a science proved the inadequacy of their consciousness.

It was not only people's flesh that was subject to decomposition. There was an intensive degradation of their mind and consciousness too. Their thought slowed down, they even lost the ability to compute sums and invented a *calculator*. They lost their ability to create holograms in space and invented a device they called a *television* — a primitive mechanism displaying something like a hologram.

They lost the ability to move themselves through space and began building artificial devices known as *cars, aeroplanes* and *spaceships.*

From time to time certain groups of people would attack other groups and they would kill each other. But, most incredible of all, the death virus gave people the notion that they were not eternal, but existed only temporarily in the space they could mentally grasp hold of.

More and more, the actions of people of the technocratic age transformed the planet Earth into a foul-smelling, smoke-stenched corner of the Universe. But the Mind of the Universe kept waiting for something, and refrained from destroying this deleterious place in the galaxy.

"Stop, please, for a moment!" Vladislav's presentation was interrupted by a voice coming from the group of his debating opponents, headed by his friend Radomir. "It's senseless to continue with your talk. It would have been impossible for something like that to happen on the Earth."

"All right, I shall break off my presentation, if you can really prove the improbability of what I have said."

From among the group of opponents one young man stood up and argued as follows:

"We have reliable reports about the existence of *religion* in Earth society. Religious treatises talked about the Earth and everything growing thereon as being created by the Mind of the Universe, which they called *God*. They worshipped him and performed many rituals in his honour. I trust, my dear presenter, that you will not deny that fact?"

"No, I shan't deny it," replied Vladislav.

"Then tell me, how could they perform rituals in honour of their god and at the same time destroy his creations? It would be impossible to do both at the same time. Consequently, these densely populated cities you speak of could not have existed on the Earth. And people could not have fouled the water created for them by the God they worshipped. In any case, the Mind of the Universe could not have countenanced such chaos, or he himself could not have been termed a 'mind'. On the contrary, it would call into question any speck of rationality in what he created — Man first and foremost. What have you to say to this, my honourable presenter?"

"I say that the existence of a Mind, especially of the Universe, is the union of two great principles — Mind and Anti-Mind.

"The age of the Anti-Mind was necessary for the people of the planet Earth. And if you will permit me, in the next part of my presentation I shall prove the existence of two great principles in Man."

"Fine, then, carry on!" the young man agreed, and sat down. Vladislav continued his presentation, now more confidently:

The world of the Universe is the union of opposites. Man also reflects this union of opposites within himself. Amidst the incredible chaos that has taken over Earth-dwellers' consciousness, all at once there appeared people capable of understanding... These people changed their attitude toward Earth's creations, but not with words and not through the aid of religious treatises. *They began to change their way of life.* While not yet fully comprehending the scope of their creation, they referred to their actions simply as 'the building of a family domain'.

They did not yet know that by approaching the Earth with a new conscious awareness, they were beginning to revitalise the planets of the Universe. They did not yet know that for them death would no longer exist, or that the children they gave birth to would be called gods by their descendants. They were simply building their family domains on the planet Earth.

In the meantime the Mind of the Universe followed their activities with trembling anticipation. And eventually the day came when all the people of the Earth began to live in their marvellous domains. And the day came when... Look, I shall show you a hologram — it has two people in it.

In the space in front of the assembly appeared a three-dimensional earthly landscape. Two elderly people, a man and a woman, were walking hand-in-hand along a pathway leading from their domain to a nearby forest. They were clearly more than a hundred years old. Evening was coming on, and the sky was filled with still barely noticeable stars. The couple walked up to a cedar tree, and the elderly woman leant her back against it.

"Here I am a grandmother now, and a great-grandmother, too," the woman tenderly remarked to her companion, "and you're still after me to go for a night-time walk under a starry sky, just like we did when we were young."

"But isn't that what you want, too?"

"Of course I do, my beloved."

He quickly grabbed her by the shoulders, gave her an impetuous hug and kissed her on the lips. Then he pushed the strap of her dress to one side, baring her shoulder. The now bright moonlight clearly revealed three birthmarks all in a row on the woman's left shoulder. The man kissed each of these in turn.

"You are just the same as you were before, my beloved, you are. I never want to part from you."

"And part we shall not. We shall die and be born anew."

"We can't afford to be born anew," she said sadly. "Just look, there's hardly any free land left on the Earth — it's all gardens and domains, everywhere you look. And it's possible our grandchildren won't have enough room. Probably the Creator failed to take this into account when He created the Earth."

"I don't think so. There is some kind of solution, but we don't know yet what it is. But I am confident that our love cannot be interrupted. You and I shall die to be born again."

"But where?"

"Look, my beloved — on that star out there! Let our thought create life anew on that planet, similar to life on the Earth. Think about it — why else would God have thought to create so many planets? It can't be just a coincidence. Our thought has a material form — it will create life for us on that lifeless planet. We shall be re-embodied again and again. Our love will be forever the same..."

"I thank you for this marvellous dream, my beloved, indeed I do. With you... I shall help you create life on that planet new."

"What shall we call it, my beloved, this planet of our new life?"

"Arreta, that's what it'll be called."

"Wait for us, Arreta! In the meantime you can blossom out in gardens and spread yourself with herbs, the way I desire," said the man, fervently and confidently.

"Me too," responded the woman.

The hologram disappeared. Vladislav bowed to the assembly and stepped off to one side, making way for his friend and opponent, Radomir.

Radomir stood in Vladislav's place, glanced around at the gathering and began to speak.

"I beg to disagree with my friend. I shall say right off: in his version of events there is a great deal that is unprovable and even contradictory. Like my friends here, I cannot believe in the existence of a period in people's history which is so utterly absurd.

"The hologram he showed, as we all realise, is only a whim of his thought and imagination and is lacking in confirmation. Though this hologram gave me a kind of strange sensation. It seemed as though my learned friend had taken it from a story already known — I just can't recall what source it is from."

A hushed whisper spread through the amphitheatre, and cries of "Plagiarism!" could be heard.

"Could it be plagiarism? Unheard of! But perhaps the presenter didn't know..."

"Plagiarism... Yes, there is a distinct impression of something we've seen before here."

Vladislav stood to one side and hung his head. He shuddered upon hearing a child's cry from one of the back rows.

"A-a-a-ah! A-a-a-ah!" his sister Katerinka kept calling out, refusing to be silenced.

At least she's just calling out, and not criticising the proceedings, thought Vladislav. But he was wrong.

After waiting for the inevitable silence to ensue, Katerinka declared in a loud voice:

"Don't even think of arguing with my big brother! 'Cause he's very, very clever and sensitive too."

"Now *there's* a weighty argument," someone said, as snickering could be heard all round.

"Quite true, very weighty indeed," little Katerinka went on. "And you, my Radomirchik, don't you go fancying Liudmila. Just don't go fancying her, and that's it!"

"Katya, keep quiet!" Vladislav cried out.

"I shan't keep quiet! Liudmilka loves you, and you love her — I know that for certain."

"Katya!" Vladislav cried out again, and headed over to where his sister was standing.

"Liudmilka, what are you sitting there for?" exclaimed Katya. "Stop him. He won't let me have my say! He'll drag me away! By force!"

A brown-haired girl rose from the back row, headed toward Vladislav and stood in his way. Liudmila's cheeks had broken out in a soft blush. With head lowered, she whispered:

"Your sister's right, Vladislav."

Her whisper could be heard through the hushed amphitheatre. All heads turned toward little Katerinka, people smiled and applauded her. Inspired by the audience's support, the little girl ran down to Radomir, who was still standing on stage. She took up a position right beside him and held up her hands to signal the gathering to quiet down.

When all were silent, she started speaking again, this time to Radomir.

"You know, Radomirchik, you almost played the traitor there. You musn't criticise my big brother. He showed everything fair and square. He's your friend. You're his friend. So don't you criticise."

Radomir glanced down condescendingly at the little girl beside him, and with equal condescension began speaking to her, as well as to the people in the amphitheatre:

"I'm not criticising. I'm simply stating a fact. There's not enough pieces of evidence in the hologram he showed. In fact, there's none."

"There is one. Or maybe two," Katerinka firmly declared.

"And where might it be — or where might *they* be, if there's two?"

"One of them is me. And the other is *you,* Radomirchik!" the little girl confidently stated.

With these words she undid two buttons on her dress and bared her shoulder. On Katerinka's left shoulder Radomir glimpsed three birthmarks, exactly the same as they had seen on the elderly Earth-woman in the hologram. Radomir examined the birthmarks on the little girl's shoulder, and his blood began rushing through his veins. He concentrated on trying to recall something. Then appeared before him a hologram which only he could see.

A country scene on the Earth. There he is, kissing the three birthmarks on his beloved's shoulder. Then she gives him a hug. She laughs and rumples his hair and kisses the end of his nose, still laughing, as usual.

The hologram disappeared.

Radomir looked for a while longer at the little girl standing in front of him, her shoulder still bared as before. Then he suddenly bent over, took Katerinka in his arms and held her close. Embracing him, she rumpled his hair and gave him a quick kiss on the end of his nose. He kept holding little Katerinka in his arms, and she whispered in his ear:

"Either you were in a hurry to be born, Radomirchik, or I was born later than I should have been. Now you must wait while I grow up. Wait fourteen years. You won't be happy with anyone else — I'm your better half!"

"I shall wait 'til you grow up, my dear," the lad responded quietly.

Exhausted by all the excitement, Katerinka now felt calmed down. She put her little head on Radomir's shoulder and fell into a sound sleep. He stood there silently before the hushed amphitheatre, carefully holding in his arms his bride-to-be.

With his mind, he began drawing letters of the alphabet in space. Those assembled read the text of the hologram he created:

THERE *IS* PROOF. IT IS IN EACH ONE OF US!
LOVE IS INFINITE AND ETERNAL IN THE UNIVERSE.

Then, slowly and carefully, so as not to awaken the little girl asleep on his shoulder, Radomir headed for the exit.

But he had forgotten to turn off the spatial expression of his thought, and so the hologram continued to sprout more letters. The audience realised that these words were not addressed to them, but they could not help reading them:

YOU RAN BAREFOOT THROUGH STARS, NOT LOOKING FOR LOVE,
AND IN NO WAY SELF-SERVING, NO NEVER.
THROUGHOUT INFINITE SPACE YOU ALONE DID PRESERVE
WHAT WE SHOULD BE PRESERVING TOGETHER.

These words were intended for a little girl of the planet Arreta, as well as for the Earth-woman — the goddess who had given life to their planet.

The little goddess slept sweetly on Radomir's shoulder. Perhaps she too was hearing in her sleep the words of her beloved.

"That's terrific, Anastasia! That means that when people follow the Divine programme and give the whole Earth a makeover, they will also have the opportunity to resettle on other planets?"

"Of course. Otherwise the very existence of other planets in the Universe would be meaningless. But He has infused everything with great meaning. The love between two people — a dream, born in love — is capable of breathing life into any planet."

"And again, Anastasia, as I understood it, the people who are now building their domains will *not* die. They will only change bodies and be reincarnated in life on the spot."

"Of course. Their actions on the Earth are more needed than anyone else's. They please God. And even people who have never managed to touch the earth with their hands, but have mentally begun to build their own future living corner of Paradise, are many times more needful to the Divine programme than hundreds of wise men sitting behind stone walls — men who have cut themselves off from God's creations, simply talking about God and spirituality.

"Their words are blasphemous and sad. Death without reincarnation awaits them. They can look forward to a fearful fate, but far from being God's punishment, this is what they have chosen as their own destiny!

"God has shone forth in the Universe with a new thought — it is not only a great energy, but a judge as well. Much has been said in treatises and legends about God's judgement. It is now coming softly and invisibly, God's judgement. It touches all the people now living on the planet. And every Man will be his own judge.

"Whoever chooses life and creates living life will be eternal and resemble the grand Creator of the Universe.

"Whoever visualises death in his imagination is doomed to death by his own thought."

It seemed as though these words of hers, spoken with a soft and confident tone on the bank of the River Ob, were taken up by the Space like an echo over the Earth. Over the past ten years I have not been the only one who has learnt how Anastasia is able to create the future through her thoughts and words.

As my boat took me further and further up the river, I could see her still standing on the shore. The Space around picked up her words on eternal life and repeated them over and over. From what galaxies, or from what worlds of the Universe, I all at once began to wonder, did Anastasia appear in her earthly likeness and impart a conscious awareness of *eternity* to the planet Earth? She is not one to lightly toss out words at random turns. And this has been confirmed in real life.

And that being the case, my dear readers, I must offer you my heartiest congratulations! On your conscious awareness! We shall live for ever, co-creating life in the Universe.

'Til our next joyful meeting, dear friends!

End of Part One

THE RINGING CEDARS SERIES AT A GLANCE

Anastasia *(ISBN 978-0-9801812-0-3)*, Book 1 of the Ringing Cedars Series, tells the story of entrepreneur Vladimir Megré's trade trip to the Siberian taiga in 1995, where he witnessed incredible spiritual phenomena connected with sacred 'ringing cedar' trees. He spent three days with a woman named Anastasia who shared with him her unique outlook on subjects as diverse as gardening, child-rearing, healing, Nature, sexuality, religion and more. This wilderness experience transformed Vladimir so deeply that he abandoned his commercial plans and, penniless, went to Moscow to fulfil Anastasia's request and write a book about the spiritual insights she so generously shared with him. True to her promise this life-changing book, once written, has become an international bestseller and has touched hearts of millions of people world-wide.

The Ringing Cedars of Russia *(ISBN 978-0-9801812-1-0)*, Book 2 of the Series, in addition to providing a fascinating behind-the-scenes look at the story of how *Anastasia* came to be published, offers a deeper exploration of the universal concepts so dramatically revealed in Book 1. It takes the reader on an adventure through the vast expanses of space, time and spirit — from the Paradise-like glade in the Siberian taiga to the rough urban depths of Russia's capital city, from the ancient mysteries of our forebears to a vision of humanity's radiant future.

The Space of Love *(ISBN 978-0-9801812-2-7)*, Book 3 of the Series, describes the author's second visit to Anastasia. Rich with new revelations on natural child-rearing and alternative education, on the spiritual significance of breast-feeding and the meaning of ancient megaliths, it shows how each person's thoughts can influence the destiny of the entire Earth and describes practical ways of putting Anastasia's vision of happiness into practice. Megré shares his new outlook on education and children's real creative potential after a visit to a school where pupils build their own campus and cover the ten-year Russian school programme in just two years. Complete with an account of an armed intrusion into Anastasia's habitat, the book highlights the limitless power of Love and non-violence.

Co-creation (ISBN 978-0-9801812-3-4), Book 4 and centrepiece of the Series, paints a dramatic living image of the creation of the Universe and humanity's place in this creation, making this primordial mystery relevant to our everyday living today. Deeply metaphysical yet at the same time down-to-Earth practical, this poetic heart-felt volume helps us uncover answers to the most significant questions about the essence and meaning of the Universe and the nature and purpose of our existence. It also shows how and why the knowledge of these answers, innate in every human being, has become obscured and forgotten, and points the way toward reclaiming this wisdom and — in partnership with Nature — manifesting the energy of Love through our lives.

Who Are We? (ISBN 978-0-9801812-4-1), Book 5 of the Series, describes the author's search for real-life 'proofs' of Anastasia's vision presented in the previous volumes. Finding these proofs and taking stock of ongoing global environmental destruction, Vladimir Megré describes further practical steps for putting Anastasia's vision into practice. Full of beautiful realistic images of a new way of living in co-operation with the Earth and each other, this book also highlights the role of children in making us aware of the precariousness of the present situation and in leading the global transition toward a happy, violence-free society.

The Book of Kin (ISBN 978-0-9801812-5-8), Book 6 of the Series, describes another visit by the author to Anastasia's glade in the Siberian taiga and his conversations with his growing son, which cause him to take a new look at education, science, history, family and Nature. Through parables and revelatory dialogues and stories Anastasia then leads Vladimir Megré and the reader on a shocking re-discovery of the pages of humanity's history that have been distorted or kept secret for thousands of years. This knowledge sheds light on the causes of war, oppression and violence in the modern world and guides us in preserving the wisdom of our ancestors and passing it over to future generations.

The Energy of Life (ISBN 978-0-9801812-6-5), Book 7 of the Series, re-asserts the power of human thought and the influence of our thinking on our lives and the destiny of the entire planet and the Universe. It also brings forth a practical understanding of ways to consciously control and build up the power of our creative thought. The book sheds still further light on the forgotten pages of humanity's history, on religion, on the roots of inter-racial and inter-religious conflict, on ideal nutrition, and shows how a new way of thinking and a lifestyle in true harmony with Nature can lead to happiness and solve the personal and societal problems of crime, corruption, misery, conflict, war and violence.

The New Civilisation (ISBN 978-0-9801812-7-2), Book 8, Part 1 of the Series, describes yet another visit by Vladimir Megré to Anastasia and their son, and offers new insights into practical co-operation with Nature, showing in ever greater detail how Anastasia's lifestyle applies to our lives. Describing how the visions presented in previous volumes have already taken beautiful form in real life and produced massive changes in Russia and beyond, the author discerns the birth of a new civilisation. The book also paints a vivid image of America's radiant future, in which the conflict between the powerful and the helpless, the rich and the poor, the city and the country, can be transcended and thereby lead to transformations in both the individual and society.

Rites of Love (ISBN 978-0-9801812-8-9), Book 8, Part 2, contrasts today's mainstream attitudes to sex, family, childbirth and education with our forebears' lifestyle, which reflected their deep spiritual understanding of the significance of conception, pregnancy, homebirth and upbringing of the young in an atmosphere of love. In powerful poetic prose Megré describes their ancient way of life, grounded in love and non-violence, and shows the practicability of this same approach today. Through the life-story of one family, he portrays the radiant world of the ancient Russian Vedic civilisation, the drama of its destruction and its re-birth millennia later — in our present time.

Vladimir Megré
The Ringing Cedars Series

Translated from the Russian by **John Woodsworth**
Edited by **Dr Leonid Sharashkin**

- Book 1 **Anastasia**
  ISBN: 978-0-9801812-0-3

- Book 2 **The Ringing Cedars of Russia**
  ISBN: 978-0-9801812-1-0

- Book 3 **The Space of Love**
  ISBN: 978-0-9801812-2-7

- Book 4 **Co-creation**
  ISBN: 978-0-9801812-3-4

- Book 5 **Who Are We?**
  ISBN: 978-0-9801812-4-1

- Book 6 **The Book of Kin**
  ISBN: 978-0-9801812-5-8

- Book 7 **The Energy of Life**
  ISBN: 978-0-9801812-6-5

- Book 8, Part 1 **The New Civilisation**
  ISBN: 978-0-9801812-7-2

- Book 8, Part 2 **Rites of Love**
  ISBN: 978-0-9801812-8-9

Published by **Ringing Cedars Press**
www.ringingcedars.com